To Rhiannon

Excellence and dedication
will always be recognized
& rewarded. You have a
great career in your
future.

Sincerely Hail
Shelley Hail
3/2016

BRICK WALL BREAKTHROUGH:
WHAT THE @#$%! DO I DO NEXT?

Actions for Exceptional
Sales and Service

by
Shelley Hall

ISBN: 978-0-9903430-0-4

Disclaimer: Although every precaution has been taken to verify the accuracy of the information contained herein, the author and publisher assume no responsibility for any errors or omissions. No liability is assumed for damages that may result from the use of the information contained within.

Permissions: Requests for permission to use any content in any manner from this book must be obtained in writing prior to such use. Permission may be requested by writing to: Shelley Hall, Catalytic Management, LLC, at shall@ catalyticmanagement.com.

Page Court Press

Praise for *Brick Wall Breakthrough!*

"A must-have book for sales leaders. A source of actionable ideas that will drive revenue and build loyal customers. If you manage salespeople or are responsible for sales strategy, *Brick Wall Breakthrough* should become your go-to resource."

– Ben Gay III, author, *The Closers*

"All at once, a read that combines theory, tools, techniques, and tips all laced with relevant humor that keeps you turning the pages, laughing, and left with a fantastic resource."

– Sue Williamson, Executive Coach,
Co-Founder, 3D Leadership

"In today's fast-paced environment, *Brick Wall Break-through* offers every manager a refreshingly easy-to-use, 'on demand' way to implement sound solutions quickly and effectively. Sales leaders and customer service managers will be energized and challenged to act! *Brick Wall Breakthrough* also comes with a bonus – a sense of humor."

– Jodi Allen, Director of Sales, Sulzer Mixpac USA

"*Brick Wall Breakthrough* will make you question long-held beliefs about sales and service that sound good in theory but don't work in reality. Shelley Hall shows you a proven process for increasing sales and delivering exceptional service. This book is a resource you will go back to time after time. *Brick Wall Breakthrough* provides a roadmap for organizations that want to increase sales growth and deliver superior customer service."

> – Susan Foley, Managing Partner, Corporate
> Entrepreneurs, LLC; author, *Entrepreneurs Inside*
> and *Acceleration: Changing the Speed of Growth*

"Shelley helps us by not only writing in an easy-to-read style, but by also using humor, applying exercises, and giving enlightening examples. For me, this book is a breakthrough all the way."

> – Dr. André A. de Waal, MBA, associate professor,
> Maastricht School of Management,
> The Netherlands, and author, *What Makes A High
> Performance Organization: Five Validated Factors
> of Competitive Advantage That Apply Worldwide*

"Shelley has done an excellent job collecting years of relevant information and presenting it in this well-written book."

> – Chris Whipple, President, Advanced Corporate Teams

"Shelley's writing is friendly, humorous, and interesting. She challenges you to take action! This is a book I'll turn to again and again."

– Joseph W. Mitchell, Jr., Senior Vice President,
Bridgewater Savings Bank

"Shelley Hall has 'nailed it' with *Brick Wall Breakthrough*. Executing her customer service advice will build customer loyalty and ultimately increase your company's profit. Her down-to-earth examples expand our understanding of the content and her wonderful humor makes it fun to read as well."

– Judi Hess, President, Customer Perspectives

To Richard

whose love, support, and encouragement have made this book
and my amazing life a reality.

BRICK WALL BREAKTHROUGH:
WHAT THE @#$%! DO I DO NEXT?

Actions for Exceptional
Sales and Service

– Table of Contents –

CUSTOMER SERVICE - ACTION DRIVERS

TALENT MANAGEMENT

CONCLUSION

– Introduction –

If you're reading this introduction, the provocative book title worked! The title, as they say, "grabbed" you. I'll bet that what *really* grabbed you is that feeling in the pit of your stomach when you think about hitting the brick wall in your business.

As a business owner – whether senior level executive, senior manager, or someone with aspirations for those titles – you've experienced that fear of "What the @#$%! do I do next?!" You're good at your job and you've enjoyed success, but now you're faced with slower-than-optimum growth, flat or declining profit margins, and/or customers and prospects that don't seem to feel the love. If you're old enough to remember seeing the first release of *Raiders of the Lost Ark*, you've faced down more than one brick wall. Or maybe you're early in your career, or just plain brilliant, and have escaped that scary experience of making the right choices when it really counts. Don't be fooled, your time is coming.

Brick Wall Breakthrough was written for you! Businesses are forever stuck in the work-in-progress mode and accepting what is necessary to maintain sanity; but that doesn't mean you have to like it. I've spent the last thirteen years as a growth consultant, working with companies big and small as they evolve in order to thrive and grow. I've witnessed great strategies in action that have bolstered growth, and I've witnessed the proverbial *"enough @#$%! on the wall"* strategy repeatedly fail.

In search of the ultimate answer, I've read hundreds of books, eBooks, journals, and white papers, made many pages of notes, and implemented strategies, simple to grand – from homegrown to Harvard Business School-worthy. In the process, I've come to realize that building, managing, and sustaining a great company takes a lot of courage, stubbornness, creativity, and – yes – the ability to work through the roadblocks.

You turned to *Brick Wall Breakthrough* looking for ideas and you'll find them here. You'll also find them quickly without the need to read an entire book. You don't have the luxury of reading 247 books, dozens of eBooks, countless journals, magazines, and white papers just to find the answer to today's challenge. The pressing issues of the day need an answer now, not days from now when you have the time and energy to pull out that great business book you were always going to read, and, well, finally attempt to read the damn thing. If only you had the ideas and answers at your fingertips. Now you do!

Brick Wall Breakthrough is designed to help you uncover the best growth strategies for your company *when* you need them. It presents highly practical, actionable ideas that have worked for me and my clients over a 30-year career as a corporate manager, business owner, and management consultant. The book is organized around the fundamental drivers of growth – sales and service – those areas of excellence you need to master in order to survive and thrive. *Brick Wall Breakthrough* is designed to be read in pieces and parts. You pull out the sections you need today and save other sections for tomorrow, next week, whenever. Call it "just-in-time advice" or "choose-your-own-adventure," but by design *Brick Wall Breakthrough* is intended for entrepreneurs and business leaders who are never content to sit back and call it "done."

As you work with the ideas and advice contained in the book, you will see a fundamental truth to *thriving*, not just surviving. That truth: become a customer-driven company. Your customers' needs should factor into virtually every business decision you make. Your first question should always be, "How will this decision, action, or strategy affect our customers? Will this new policy, process, product, or partnership support the needs, wants, and goals of our customers?" When you can answer "yes," you've chosen the right path.

– How to Use *Brick Wall Breakthrough* –

You're a busy CEO, business owner, or senior manager. You rarely have the luxury of reading all those business management books lining your bookshelf. That's why *Brick Wall Breakthrough* guides you with **Action Drivers** – those selling and customer service skills and actions that drive growth. Action Drivers are presented under the major growth components of Sales, Customer Service, and Talent Management.

Action Driver topics include:

- Effective Selling
- Superior Customer Service
- Quality Talent Management

Each Action Driver topic will present practical ideas, suggestions, warnings, and wisdom related to that topic. At the conclusion of each Action Driver section, you will find a **Deep Dives** resource list of relevant, valuable books for when you have the time or the need to delve deeper into a specific topic.

Finally, you'll find a **Fast Finder** index at the conclusion of the book. The Fast Finder index is organized by business challenges, making it easier to find just-in-time solutions to your pressing challenge.

Use *Brick Wall Breakthrough* as a tool to drive your employees' participation in developing the strategies and tactics that accelerate and foster continuous growth. There it is – your first truism in growing your department, division, or company: **Growth is a team sport!**

SALES

– The Sales Cycle –

Value Stream Map Your Sales Process

Sales executives are consistently told to "rebuild your sales process to match your customer's buying process." Sound advice to shorten your sales cycle, but how to get it done? By deploying **Value Stream Mapping** you can create a visual plan of your current sales process, your customer's buying process, and then compare the two. Value Stream Mapping is a tool most often used by manufacturing companies implementing LEAN manufacturing principles. But this graphical tool is increasingly deployed to examine non-manufacturing processes such as order entry, shipping, product development, and customer service. The foundation of Value Stream Mapping is to identify "waste" in your process, defined as activity that does not add value for your customer. Applying the principle to a sales process can do more than just eliminate waste – it can help you:

- Reconfigure a sales process to more closely resemble how your customer buys
- Identify "customer touch points" where marketing can enhance the process
- Identify decision points, thus giving your sales team time to influence the criteria and the final decision
- Build a skills/competency model for your sales team
- Increase efficiency, thereby reducing costs and improving margins
- Increase revenue through a higher closing ratio

Brick Wall Breakthrough

There are two aspects to undertaking a Value Stream Mapping initiative that must be addressed: **designing a project plan**, and **understanding how to build a Value Stream Map**.

Designing the Project Plan

In designing a project plan, using the basic framework of another process tool, **Six Sigma**, will keep the project on track and insure success. The steps of the Six Sigma methodology are:

Define: Define your different customer segments. Examine them for buying differences and select the segment that either most closely resembles the norm or represents your highest margin contribution, then focus on this group. Once identified, invite two or more customers in this segment to participate in a joint Value Stream Mapping of their buying/decision process. They benefit in two ways: by building a better process through highlighting methods to eliminate waste, and by having a partner who is willing to change its selling process to make buying from them easier (note: focus on one customer at a time).

Measure: In this step the goal is to objectively examine and understand current buying and selling processes and their performance. Using Value Stream Mapping, you will map your customer's current buying process and your current selling process. During this phase you should focus on the reality, not what you want the process to be. Focus on what it is without judgment.

Analyze: Analyze the buying process map with your customer to identify redundant activities, rework, multiple approvals or reviews, and gaps where the process slows downs. The goal is to work with your customer to improve his buying process while you gain insight into how to make your sales process mirror it. Upon completion of the analysis, you should create a **Future Buying Process** map that will become the customer's new and improved method of buying.

Improve: Improvement now focuses on your selling process. Examine your selling process in comparison to the new future map of your customer's buying process and the variances and differences will become obvious. You are likely to see that you have placed emphasis on the wrong steps in the selling process. You'll see where the customers may wait for you to take action and, thus, where you slow their buying process. Armed with the knowledge of where your process doesn't align with that of your customer, you can now reconfigure your sales process to streamline the activities and get to "yes!" faster and more efficiently.

Control: The new selling process should be documented and the sales team should receive training in skills that may now have increased in importance based on the critical touch points of the buying and selling process. Your CRM and Customer Data Management (CDM) systems should be customized to accommodate, support, and speed the new selling process.

Define Start and End of Process

Current State Map Sales and Buying Processes

Analyze and Compare Sales and Buying Processes

Rebuild Sales Processes to Reflect Buying Process

Create Future State Map of Sales Process

Brick Wall Breakthrough

The Tool: Value Stream Mapping

Value Stream Mapping is the critical tool used in measuring and analyzing your selling process and your customer's buying process. Value Stream Mapping is a more in-depth version of a process flow chart. The addition of mapping the communication flow in a Value Stream Map distinguishes it from a process flow map and gives it additional value over the basic process flow. Don't listen to the skeptic who will tell you that Value Stream Mapping is overly complicated and beyond what you need. In the hands of experts, it can be. But there is no need to make the project difficult; even a simple Value Stream map will help you rebuild your sales process to parallel your customer's buying process. Below are some suggestions on how to approach the mapping project:

1. Create your own **Current State Map** of your sales process before you work with your client. The practice will be invaluable and will help you assess the variances in the two processes as you conduct the mapping with your client.

2. **Reinforce that you want the reality** when creating the Current State Map – not how people think the process is supposed to work – but how it actually does work now.

3. Assure your staff that **truth-telling will be rewarded** but finger-pointing will be punished.

4. Select a **mapping team** to list the high level steps in the process and then do much of the detail in a spreadsheet before creating the pictorial map. For instance, type each high level step into a separate spreadsheet cell, then ask each person involved in the process to enter what activities they perform into the cells below the step.

5. Once you have used the spreadsheets to create the Current State Map for your sales process, **repeat this process with your customers** to create their buying process maps.

6. **Analyze where your sales process varies** from the customer's buying process. For instance, if your customer needs product or service specs earlier than your process currently produces them, then you have found an opportunity to adjust your process to provide what your customer needs *when* they need it.

7. When your analysis of the variances is complete, create a proposed **Future State Map** of the new sales process. Use this map to "beta test" the process with the customer before you pull the plug on the current process.

The greatest value of Value Stream Mapping is its view of the Communication Flow: it's always ripe for improvement. Once you have created the new sales process, take things one step further and add the Communication Flow to the process map (this flow is depicted above the main process flow blocks). My bet is you will find several "Aha!" moments when you look at how the strings of communication resemble a plate of spaghetti. This is your opportunity to improve internal efficiencies by reducing approvals or reviews, eliminating rework, combining information, and generally reducing the back and forth of communication as much as possible.

Creating a sales and marketing process that mirrors your customer's buying process will shorten the cycle, increase your closing percentage, reduce sales team frustration, and create very happy long-term customers. Value Stream Mapping is the perfect tool to accomplish this.

– Lead Generation –

Potato/Potahto, Tomato/Tomahto!
Is It an Inquiry or a Lead?

Communication is more than how we pronounce a word; it's about our definition of a word – you say potato, I say potahto, let's call the whole thing off! In the words of George and Ira Gershwin, this little ditty sums up the debate on when is a lead a lead? Is the request for your brochure really a lead? Is leaving a business card in your bowl at a trade show really a lead? Is filling out your website contact form to receive a white paper a lead? And does the definition of a lead affect the actions of your sales team? Is it a potato or pot*ah*to?

Well, I say POTAHTO! The above examples are not leads; they are *inquiries*. According to a Harvard Business Study, 80% of leads never receive follow up from the sales team. Why? Because what the sales team gets are, more often than not, just inquiries. If you give your team those business cards from the trade show or a list of website form names and ask them to follow up, you're setting up both yourself and your sales team for failure. So, what do you do to turn inquiries into revenue? Change your mind set; and:

- Accept the difference between an inquiry and a lead.
- **Differentiate the terms**: an *inquiry* has expressed an *interest* in your product or service, while a *lead* is an inquiry that has been

contacted, profiled, and qualified according to specific business criteria like purchase time frame or needs match.

- Define your process from **Inquiry to Qualified Lead** to **Qualified Prospect to Sale** (see Impact Score Card on page 13).
- Assign the qualification stage in the process to your inside sales team. **Don't have an inside sales team then outsource the qualification** or assign it to a marketing person. Don't waste your professional selling team on the qualification step UNLESS you are selling a one-off or commodity product that can and should be done in one prospect interaction.
- **Score and categorize** the inquiry based on specific, defined criteria and then distribute according to those categories.

Let's examine these steps more closely. First, start with the right definitions: an **inquiry** is when someone has expressed interest in your product or service; a **lead** is an inquiry that has been contacted, profiled, and qualified according to defined criteria based on your company's target customer.

Second, create a process for shepherding the inquiry into becoming a qualified prospect:

Generate Inquiry:	Via marketing, advertising, trade shows, web, networking, etc.
Capture Inquiry:	Capture basic information and enter it into the CRM system.

First Level Qualification:	The inquiry is contacted, scored, and qualified based on a defined set of criteria specific to your company Inquiry becomes a lead.
Assignment:	The lead is prioritized based on the score, then assigned based on the action categories of sell, nurture, discard.
Second Level Qualification:	Sales contacts the initially-qualified lead directly and conducts both a needs and a readiness-to-purchase assessment. This is an in-depth qualification; the lead could change categories after this conversation.
Close the Sale:	The "selling process" begins as the lead becomes a qualified prospect.
Analysis:	The entire process is assessed and metrics are established: i.e., cost-per-inquiry, per-qualified-lead, per-sale, etc.

Based on this process, there are four questions you must answer:

1. **Who** conducts the first level qualification?

2. **What criteria** should be used to score and qualify the inquiry?

3. **What process to nurture** the "not ready to purchase" inquiries or leads do you have? Remember the difference between an *inquiry* and a *lead* – an inquiry only becomes a lead if it meets specific criteria. After the Second Level of Qualification, a lead may still not be ready to purchase and thus needs to be nurtured.

4. **What process to capture** and use the resulting statistics do you have in place? This is a critical component. Understanding what

is going on with your inquiry generation and lead management is critical to making changes or adjustments to the process because it is not driving revenue.

First Level Qualification. Who conducts the first level qualification is a very important decision. While the qualification activity obviously is critical, it is equally important to note that the real act of selling is not, and probably should not, take place at this point. Therefore, should your most skilled and expensive sales talent perform the qualification? No. Utilize your less-costly (but not necessarily less-talented) personnel to qualify the inquiry and, once qualified, pass the lead onto the sales team.

Scoring and Categorizing the Inquiry. A score based on specific criteria should be established and used as a way to categorize inquiries. Your sales and marketing teams should jointly develop the criteria based on your ideal prospect (see Impact Scorecard Tool on page 13).

Once you have scored the inquiry, it should be assigned to one of three categories: **sell, nurture,** or **discard**. Your professional sales team assumes responsibility for the sell Action Driver; marketing assumes the responsibility for the nurturing process.

Converting the Lead into an Appointment. If you have determined that the inquiry is qualified and is now a true lead, then the first step in selling, i.e., securing the appointment, becomes by nature the most important step. Yet converting leads into an appointment is often the Achilles heel of a sales team. Before picking up the phone, your sales team should ask these questions:

1. Why should the lead/prospect buy my product or service?

2. Why should it grant me an appointment now versus three months from now?

3. What is my real goal in following up on this lead?

The answer to that last question is to secure an appointment – period. Securing an appointment is all about four things:

1. Uncovering why the prospect was interested.

2. Translating that interest into a need that should be solved *sooner* rather than later.

3. Translating the understanding of the prospect's need into an appropriate value offering, i.e., a solution.

4. Asking for the appointment in a manner that indicates that you *both need to assess each other.*

Changing your mindset to accept the difference between an inquiry and a lead is the first step in converting inquires to leads to sales. Being honest and realistic about how you qualify, score, categorize, and assign those inquiries will increase your overall sales, improve the quality of your sales, shorten your sales cycle, and reduce your cost of sales.

– Lead Generation –

ACTION DRIVER ▶ *Impact Score Card*

IMPACT SCORE© Inquiry Assessment & Qualification Tool

Catalytic Management developed **IMPACT SCORE©** to help our clients consistently quantify the value of an inquiry. We believe that using a systematic, quantitative approach like this will help eliminate expensive follow-through on low-value inquiries, prioritize your existing inquiries, and best measure the results of business development activities.

1. Evaluate your company's strategic priorities

2. Inventory your prospect's priorities related to this purchase.

3. Integrate your findings to produce your IMPACT SCORE

4. Apply this scoring method to all inquiries in order to generate an intelligent "sell-nurture-discard" action list.

1. EVALUATE WHAT MATTERS MOST TO YOUR SALES STRATEGY

The first step involves quantifying high-value prospects. Begin by reviewing the four criteria below, weighing each based on how important those criteria are to your business or segment.

Defining the importance of each criterion will depend on the current sales and marketing strategy. For example, if driving revenue quickly is most important, then give a higher weight to the "purchase time" and "budget" criteria. If, however, the goal is to open a new market or secure a large reference account, then over-weight the "strategic value to your company" criterion.

Keep in mind that all four assigned weightings percentages must add up to 100%.

1. _____% **Need/Solution** How important is the solution/product to the prospect's company and goals?

_____% **Purchase Time Frame** How quickly is a purchase expected?

_____% **Budget** Has a budget been established? Is the solution within their budget constraints?

_____% **Strategic Value Company** Does this lead have high value?

_____
100%

IMPACT SCORE© Inquiry Assessment & Qualification Tool

2. EVALUATE WHAT MATTERS MOST TO YOUR PROSPECT

Consider the same four criteria but this time with consideration of the prospect's stated priorities related to this purchase. What drives the prospect's decision-making? Consult the scoring table below and score the prospect within each criterion.

Need/Solution

100	Strong need: your company has a unique solution
75	Strong need: few vendors to buy from
50	Need but not vital
25	Can purchase anywere

Budget

100	Budget is approved
75	Budget is in approval process
50	Can secure money outside budget
25	Will need to "find" money

Strategic Value to Company

100	Large account; exceptional potential/new market
75	Will bring other accounts with it
50	High margins
25	Revenue driver only

Purchase Time Frame

100	0 to 3 months
75	3 to 6 months
50	6 to 12 months
25	Longer than 12 months

EVALUATION OF PROSPECT BASED ON THE SCORING SYSTEM ABOVE

_____ Need/Solution   _____ Purchase Time Frame

_____ Budget   _____ Strategic Value to Company

---

3. MULTIPLY THE INTERNAL AND PROSPECT SCORES TO CREATE A PRIORITY LIST

Now you must take the weightings from Step 1 and multiply them by the prospect evaluation from Step 2. This will score the prospect and determine the true value of the inquiry and reveal what action must be taken. The table below shows a sample prospect.

3. YOUR PROSPECT SCORE AND RECOMMENDED ACTION (for example only)

	STEP 1 WEIGHT	STEP 2 EVALUATION		STEP 3 SCORE
NEED/SOLUTION	10%	85		8.50
BUDGET	25%	75		18.75
STRATEGIC VALUE TO COMPANY	15%	50	X	7.50 =
PURCHASE TIME FRAME	50%	75		37.50
SAMPLE PROSPECT SCORE				72.25

IMPACT SCORE© Inquiry Assessment & Qualification Tool

4 How to use the IMPACT SCORE tool with a large grouping of prospects/inquiries.

Now that the individual prospect has been scored, you can use this knowledge to create an automatic scoring system for all your prospects, whether in an Excel spreadsheet or by embedding the information into existing CMS program(s).

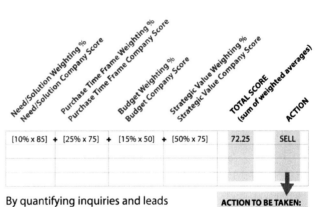

ABC Company
Green Industries LLC
Partners, Inc.
Brown & Brown, LLC

	Need/Solution Weighting % Need/Solution Company Score	Purchase Time Frame Weighting % Purchase Time Frame Company Score	Budget Weighting % Budget Company Score	Strategic Value Weighting % Strategic Value Company Score	TOTAL SCORE (sum of weighted averages)	ACTION
ABC Company	[10% x 85] +	[25% x 75] +	[15% x 50] +	[50% x 75]	72.25	SELL
Green Industries LLC						
Partners, Inc.						
Brown & Brown, LLC						

By quantifying inquiries and leads into a sustainable, consistent program, resources can be apportioned appropriately and more time can be spent on the most valuable, attractive business leads.

ACTION TO BE TAKEN:	
>50	SELL
30 – 50	NURTURE
<30	DISCARD

– Customer Relationship Management –

ACTION DRIVER ▶ *But They Said It Would Wash My Car While I Was Driving Home!*

Two years ago, we installed a brand-new, high-energy-efficient boiler with the superstore hot water heater. The price was double what a normal boiler would cost, but it was "The Best Boiler." The heating company justified the cost with statements and promises like:

- Your energy bill will decrease by 30%!
- You'll have more precise control of room temperature!
- You'll never run out of hot water!
- You'll lose 20 pounds and look ten years younger! (OK - they didn't say that but they came close)

Needless to say, very little of what they promised was true. What <u>was</u> true was that the installation was time-consuming and complicated. What <u>was</u> true is that we needed "training" on how to use the damn thing. What <u>was</u> true was that this new system was delicate, i.e., temperamental. *Two days* after the warranty expired, the motherboard failed. $1,200 later we had a new motherboard, but only after incurring $600 in charges to replace other parts in an effort to diagnose the situation. As to the claim of money saving: well, yes, The Best Boiler has saved us money, but only because the price of gas has dropped precipitously. My gas usage, however, has changed very little.

Brick Wall Breakthrough

So, when I hear about companies getting ready to install the latest and greatest CRM system, my horror story about The Best Boiler always comes to mind: beware of the promises you hear!

CRM implementations fail every day and it is often due to unrealistic expectations set by the software manufacturer. Installing a CRM system does not make your sales problems go away. In many instances, CRM installs will cause more upfront problems than you had hoped it would solve. Here's why - these common misconceptions and unrealistic expectations are the root of many failures.

CRM Falsehoods:

- CRM will force the sales team to follow our processes and document their client work
- CRM will improve the performance of our under-performing sales reps
- CRM is software, therefore the project should be managed by IT
- CRM will insure that our marketing programs are effective
- CRM will force Sales and Marketing to work seamlessly together
- CRM systems are relatively simple and intuitive and our staff can learn the system on its own

CRM Truths:

Fix Your Sales Process First: Leading CRM vendors often sell the hype that installing their solution will organize your sales chaos and give managers instant dashboard reports that tell the true story. WRONG! Remember the old adage: garbage in–garbage out!

You must carefully examine all aspects of your existing sales and marketing processes. Throw out the worst elements of the process, fix the broken elements, and improve the rest <u>before</u> you even start the CRM vendor evaluation process. CRM systems start out generic but, in order to insure that your CRM efforts are successful, you must customize the vendor's systems to <u>your</u> processes – not the other way around. And, your processes must be effective from the start. CRM is one of the most important examples of getting it right the first time!

CRM considerations should begin with a strong commitment to business process improvement techniques and tools. Build flow charts of your processes within and across departments to understand where the breakdowns occur; then fix them. Use your process maps to evaluate CRM vendors. Give them your sales process maps and ask them to demonstrate how their systems will mirror and support your processes.

And don't forget your customers! Your CRM system must be as simple or as complex as your customers. This is a unique opportunity to involve key customers in defining your new CRM system – don't pass it up!

<u>"Out-of-the-Box" is Bull</u>: If a CRM salesman tells you his system will work out-of-the-box with little to no customization, he is only correct if all you need is an online rolodex. Every CRM system out there needs customization, whether minor or massive, to get aligned with your goals and sales  process. Customization is not even possible unless you have mapped your sales process, have very clear metrics you want to measure, and have understood the compromises you will need to make.

Brick Wall Breakthrough

<u>Systems Don't Change Users – Users Work the System!</u> Even the best CRM system will not solve your performance issues. Poor performing sales people will be poor users of your CRM system. It may make it easier for management to identify poor performers and, after time, you may discover who has been manipulating the system, but trying to fix "broken" sales people is just as bad as installing a CRM to fix your broken sales processes. What's more, it's also important to realize that, in many aspects, CRM systems measure <u>past</u> activities and are not as good at predicting <u>future</u> ones.

And don't count on a CRM system to cure any problems between Sales and Marketing. Department relationships are created, thwarted, or sabotaged by people. A CRM system can be a great weapon in that war, but building and sustaining cross-functional support requires effective department managers.

<u>Work in Parallel</u>: Never, never, **absolutely never turn off, remove, or otherwise disable your current system until you have run the new system in parallel**. If the new CRM isn't working, you can go back to the old one <u>only</u> if it's still there! Believe me, I have clients who have given up on the new system out of sheer frustration and so returned to what worked before.

<u>Sales and Marketing *Must* Own the CRM Initiative</u>: You should look to IT for help in determining and evaluating systems against their technical standards, but IT cannot dictate your solution. This is absolutely a case where the "user buyer," i.e., Sales and Marketing, must carry more weight then the "technical buyer." If your company culture gives IT all authority over software purchases and installations, be prepared to do battle for the right CRM system. This is not the time to be pennywise and pound foolish and go for the least expensive system because it will make the

IT Department's life less complicated. My outlook is this: you are IT's customer! Its role is to insure that you are happy and your needs are met, not vice versa.

Doing your homework up front and improving your sales and marketing processes will give you the information you need to clearly define the right system; clearly-defined systems requirements will provide the leverage you need with IT. Return-on-Investment (ROI) calculations will also provide compelling leverage to secure the right solution. Sales and Marketing must own the systems from the beginning and should continue to drive upgrades and additional customization to meet their needs and their customer's needs.

Adoption and Execution are Change Management Issues: Ignore the human dynamics and "dramatics" in CRM initiatives at your peril! CRM is not "build it and they will come." People in general – and sales people in particular – will resist change, even when it's in their best interest. So be sure to start by demonstrating that it is in their best interest! Involve Sales and Marketing staff in setting the system specifications. Get your sales team to talk to customers and solicit their wants and needs. Resist the urge to focus on how CRM will generate revenue and activity reports for sales management. Instead, focus on how much easier it will be for the sales team to track customers from needs identification to closure. Talk about how the team will, at a glance, be able see who the players are within the complex sales process, as well as how to develop an appropriate strategy to lead them to the sale.

And train and train and train again! Training should be a journey, not a single event! Train on segments of the system rather than the whole in order to give people time to master that segment before moving on. Force feeding the new system in one sitting is a recipe for disaster. And never assume that any system is simple enough for the team to learn on its own.

Companies derive great benefit from carefully planned and executed CRM initiatives when their expectations are realistic and they take the time to:

- Map and reengineer the sales process
- "Sell the benefits" of the system to critical users
- Assign ownership to Sales and Marketing
- Train, train, train

Prepare, plan, plan again, and build in emergency contingencies before you buy and install the latest and greatest CRM system. Remember, failure is not an option.

– Customer Relationship Management –

ACTION DRIVER ▶ *You Can't Build Your Parachute on the Way Down: 10 Questions to Ask*

Truly effective CRM systems are built around your needs and your sales processes. Before you even begin to evaluate your CRM options, you need to know the answer to the following ten questions in order to assess just how well the vendor's solution meets your needs:

1. Are your sales defined as *simple* or *complex*? Are multiple departments within the prospect or client involved in the sale? How many decision makers must you convince?

2. Have you developed a customer profile that includes whether:

   a. Your customer has multiple buyers?
   b. Your customer has multiple divisions that are also potential sales opportunities?
   c. Your client has dispersed domestic and or international divisions?

3. Do your customers require customization of your products or services?

4. Are you selling a commodity? If yes, how do you position your company against the competition? With faster delivery? Flexible pricing?

5. Do you have individual sales reps or are you structured around account teams? Do you have local and national account managers? Do you divide sales teams into "farmers" and "hunters"? By geography? Industry? The alphabet?

6. How long or complicated is your sales cycle?

7. Can your customers order directly without the involvement of a sales person? Or do you sell through distributors or contract reps?

8. What customer service elements make you competitive? Do you need to improve service in order to improve profits?

9. What do your competitors do that you should emulate or perfect?

10. How do you expect Marketing and Sales to work together?

Spend some time thinking about the answers to these ten questions. Then share them with each CRM vendor and require that they address your answers/your needs in their demonstrations and proposals.

– Discovery Questioning –

 *Don't Ask, Don't Tell*

In the context of the military, this phrase meant personnel should not ask about a soldier's personal life and soldiers should keep their private lives, well, private. This policy was finally moth-balled in 2011. **But in sales, Don't Ask, Don't Tell has a whole different meaning.**

In sales, "Don't Ask, Don't Tell" means: "If you didn't ask the right discovery questions to uncover the client's needs, then you haven't earned the right to tell them about your product or service."

Taking it a step further, you're not practicing consultative selling if you let the client alone define his need. The client obviously knows he has a need or he wouldn't have taken the time to meet with you. But, your value should be in defining that need <u>and</u> in highlighting the *depth* of the need. The prospect's or client's ability to articulate a need and a solution is not an indication that he is right.

"I hear you!" you're saying, "But I always ask discovery questions. I'm a damn good sales diagnostician!" Maybe, but not all questions are equal. The right questioning should create a real dialogue that goes beyond the typical questions the client has likely already heard. The best discovery questions focus on **comparison**. You need to probe beyond the typical questions like: Tell me about your challenge? How has the process been working? What would it be worth to you to fix the problem?

Let's look at an example. I worked with a company that said it needed customer service training because its customers were complaining. I started the discovery process with good questions like:

- What have you done to improve service?
- Why do you think service is worse?
- What are your customers specifically telling you about your service?

When I focused on comparison questions, the real root of the service decline became apparent. We probed further by asking a comparison question:

- Tell me how the staff currently behaves and how that behavior differs from that of two years ago?
- What has changed during that time?

The last question hit the jackpot! The owner of the company had retired and a new president was hired. This critical knowledge led to these comparison questions:

- How would you compare how the staff behaves toward your customers and how they behave toward each other?
- How was the company's culture before the owner's retirement compared to now with the new president?

The root of the decline in service quality was a new negative company culture, something no amount of customer service training was going to change. By asking comparison questions, I helped the client see what it hadn't seen before. We prevented the client from implementing a solution that wouldn't solve its problem.

Don't leave money on the table or deliver the wrong solution because you're not asking the right questions. Become an expert at asking the questions that get your client to see past the obvious symptoms of the pain into the root of that pain. You need to get the client to the "Aha!" moment.

Selling is a complicated skill and sales managers are always trying to focus on key skills when managing their teams for success. Every aspect of your particular selling process is important and weakness in one area will naturally reduce your closing percentage.

But the most important step in the selling process is *discovery questioning*. Any lawyer will tell you that the "discovery phase" is the key to making their case. They must ask not only the right questions, but those that get the witness to say more than he intended. In sales, many call this the "Needs Analysis" step; but just determining the need is not enough. If you want to improve your service/product presentation as a sales manager, build deeper relationships with prospects and clients, and close more business, then focus the lion's share of your energy into building the discovery questioning skills of your sales team.

Here are ten reasons why becoming a superstar at discovery is worth the time and effort. Great discovery questions will:

1. Help the prospect see problems or challenges it didn't realize existed, thus broadening your possible solution.

2. Frame the conversation around solutions and so create the image that your company solves problems and doesn't just push products or services.

3. Determine how to customize your service/product presentation, focusing on the benefits and solutions that are the most relevant and most important to the customer.

4. Establish your salespeoples' credibility by demonstrating their understanding of the prospect's industry or market.

5. Provide an opportunity to assess the prospect's buying and communication style so presentations and proposals are targeted to how he wishes to receive and process information.

6. Uncover the client's decision criteria and who its decision-makers are.

7. Establish the consequences of inaction for the prospect.

8. Give you a glimpse at a client's potential objections and the opportunity to address them early in the conversation.

9. Explore the value and/or importance of solving the problem.

10. Begin the closing process much earlier in the conversation, i.e., closing becomes a foregone conclusion.

Really deep and effective discovery does all of the above and more if your sales reps ask before they tell. Any sales conversation – I repeat, any sales conversation – should focus on the prospect or client first. You can't customize your presentation to their specific needs if you don't first ask. You can't tailor your value proposition to match its value definition if you tell first, then ask. If your sales people are giving the product/service spiel first, your chances of closing the sale just dropped dramatically.

Don't be fooled when your sales people tell you they always ask first and that they are good at uncovering needs. Find out if they're right; ride with them and listen to how they managed the discovery process. Be sure they are asking comparison questions, those that dig deeper than the typical "what kinds of insurance have you had in the past?" Your team should be asking, "What has changed since you last purchased insurance? How would you compare your risk tolerance today to what it was five years ago? Why do you think it has or has not changed?"

Coach your sales reps to move beyond superficial discovery questions. Coach them in your sales meetings and on the road. Sales meetings should always have an educational component. For your next sales meeting, create prospect scenarios and have the team role play asking discovery questions. Or, as a team, ask reps to list the discovery questions they would ask a specific prospect. Create a prospect scenario that includes the discovery questions that should be asked, with answers the prospect might give. Then ask that salesperson to customize her sales presentation based on the prospect's answers. As sales manager, teach your team the importance of discovery with consistent education and focus.

Great discovery questions fall into five categories:

1. **Circumstance questions** are superficial but necessary. They are focused on getting the facts about a situation or collecting data such as surveys or revenue figures.

2. **Challenge questions** begin to reveal problems: challenges and dissatisfactions. The client is generally pretty good at telling you about some of their challenges, but the key is to discover if those are challenges or symptoms of a root issue.

3. **Consequence questions** begin to help the client explore the impact or implications of a problem.

4. **Comparison questions** help both you and the client analyze changes that may go unnoticed over time but which could be at the root of the problem.

5. **Value-Benefit** questions get the client to see the value of solving the problem and the urgency to do so.

Here's how a series of good discovery questions might look. These were developed for a health cancer screening program with the goal of securing more support and involvement from physicians and health care centers.

Discovery Question Type	Sample Questions
Circumstance Questions that gather data, background facts	• Do you know your current colorectal cancer screening rates? • What percentage of your patients are 50 or over? • How is your office organized?
Challenges Questions that uncover problems, dissatisfactions	• How do you currently promote screening? • What percentage of your patients follow through with your recommendation to get screened? • What roadblocks do you face in following up with patients?
Consequences Questions that explore consequences of a problem	• How would increasing your screening rate impact your quality measures? • What happens if your patients don't heed your advice? • What would it mean to you and your patients to know your screening is below average?
Comparison Questions that explore what has changed, uncover root causes	• In the two years since you have implemented the new tracking system, what has changed? • How would you compare screening rates from three years ago to today? • How would you compare your current staff's commitment to screening to that of the staff you had two years ago?
Value Questions that explore the value or importance of solving a problem	• If we could make it easy for you to raise your screening rates, would that be valuable? • If we could help you deliver better care to cancer patients, would you see that as important?

Good sales people will create a list of discovery questions before they leave the office for an appointment. They will be sure to include questions under each of the discovery categories above. Developing the list in advance ensures that a salesperson is focusing on the answers during the client conversation, not thinking about what should be asked next. When you ride with your sales people, ask to see their discovery questions. Work with them on including questions under each Action Driver and coach them through a custom presentation based on potential answers. As Sales Manager, the best use of your time is in coaching your team for excellence and improving the team's discovery skills. You will increase your closing percentage and thus increase revenue, the ultimate goal of any sales manager.

– Discovery Questioning –

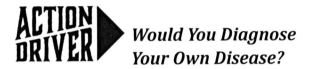 *Would You Diagnose Your Own Disease?*

Cut to TV commercial: Man is sitting at his kitchen table with a knife in front of him and a phone in his hand. You hear his doctor say, "Now make a two-inch incision just below the sternum." The patient at the kitchen table asks, "Shouldn't you be doing this?"

Excellent question. Shouldn't your sales team be diagnosing your client's problems, prescribing the correct solution, then working with the client to implement the solution? After all, sales reps are the subject matter experts!

Ah, I can hear you say, "YES! Our sales team does that." We drill them in conducting needs analyses as part of the selling process. We teach them that asking the customer questions about its problems is the first step in a meeting. We beat our sales people about the head until they can recite the mantra that our solutions are unique to the prospect's situation; that's where we deliver value to the prospect or customer.

But is your sales team uncovering the real client issues? Or is it merely asking clients to "share" their challenges? Is the team listening for what the client wants, and not what the client *needs*?

Brick Wall Breakthrough

Almost every client has thought about its challenges and very likely has internally discussed a solution. The mere act of calling you – or answering your call – is an indication that the client has at least framed a solution and they think you have that solution. Sales people – and through them, your company – add value, <u>real</u> value, only when they question the client's assumptions. The value you offer is in holding up the mirror for the client to see its real problems, to see the depth of its challenges. Human nature is such that being honest about our problems is difficult at best, and the greatest service you can provide for a prospect or client is to act as the lens through which it can filter the real from the obvious, the hard from the easy.

Differentiating your company from the competition begins when your sales team probes beyond the superficial discovery questions. Uncovering the underlying problems is a multi-layered questioning technique.

Children are expert at getting to the root cause. How many times have you heard, "But Daddy – why is the grass green?" You reply with a valid scientific answer and your child's response is, "But why?" Kids can seemingly go on forever with the WHY? It is this kind of probing, going beyond the client's first explanation, that roots out the real cause and gives the sales person the data he or she needs to develop lasting and truly unique solutions.

Now you're saying, "Boy, she doesn't have much respect for the intelligence of our clients. She obviously doesn't think clients are capable of assessing their own problems." Wrong. I have great respect for my prospects and clients, and because of that respect I believe I owe them more than just superficial answers. The client called me because my company is the expert; if I fail to share my experience and expertise, I fail the client.

Making the sale because you gave the prospect what it wanted is nothing to brag about – that's easy; your competition can do that too. But, if you made the sale because the client gained a deeper under-standing of its challenges through you – now that's something to brag about! Conducting conversations with prospects and clients at this higher, deeper level builds credibility, demonstrates a true customer focus, and in the end earns more sales.

Need proof that clients are not always right about the root cause of their problem? My company was asked to work with a software company whose VP of Sales felt the team wasn't closing enough business. We were asked to find out why, but were told over and over again that the VP believed the team needed to be more aggressive and needed training in closing. In discussions with the client, we convinced him that a real assessment should be conducted and should include interviews with clients. Well, what do you know! The client's diagnosis of the problem was way off base – his clients explained that, due to increased competition, our client's pricing was out of line with the market and that our client's poor marketing materials weren't selling its unique benefits. Training his team in closing techniques was the VP's solution, but it turned out to be the wrong solution because closing was not the problem. In order to close more business, his team needed competitive pricing, improved marketing, better positioning, and a compelling value offering.

Teach your sales people to be old-fashioned detectives. Never take anything at face value. Always look for the links between pieces of evidence. Ask the same question three different ways. The television formula for detective series, medical shows, and mysteries teach us that what seems obvious is just a ruse. The real criminal or diagnosis is layers deep. Sales people add value when they add insight and perspectives that the prospect or client can't find internally.

– Selling Your Value –

ACTION DRIVER ▶ *From Socrates to Snooki:*
Celestial Heavens vs. Tattoos

You're thinking I've lost my mind! How can I put Socrates and Snooki in the same sentence? One is a respected Greek philosopher and the other a hard-to-watch party girl from the reality TV series *Jersey Shore*. They are as different as night and day, and it is just that difference that matters in selling.

Over the years I have worked with clients who have difficulty articulating their value proposition. Here's a tip: there is no one value statement! Just as beauty is in the eye of the beholder, value is what the prospect or customer decides it is! Value can be very personal, and the greatest sales people find out what their prospect or customer values before presenting their product or service.

Let's say you sell Celestron™ telescopes and you're trying to get Socrates and Snooki to each buy your new AstroMaster 114 EQ. You can tell them both that Celestron is a leader in designing optical products, that the AstroMaster is <u>the</u> telescope of choice for the discerning consumer, offering lens magnification of 165X, and a stellar magnitude of 11.7.

While these features have overall value, features are not value nor benefits, and they won't get your AstroMaster 114 EQ sold. Why? Because

Brick Wall Breakthrough

Socrates wants a telescope for celestial viewing, and Snooki wants to zoom in on the tattoo of the gorgeous guy across the street while he's in the shower.

If you really want to sell a telescope, tailor your value proposition to the value definition of your prospect. Your respective value statements should be:

"The AstroMaster 114 EQ will deliver clear, crisp images of all the stars in the Milky Way and deep space." Socrates says, "Where might I signeth?"

"If you want to zoom in on some ripped abs and a tight butt, the AstroMaster will get it done." After uttering an expletive, Snooki screams "Butt cheeks, here I come!"

Learning your prospect's personal definition of value is the key to the sale. But how do you find that out? You ask! You "discover" by asking questions. Develop then ask a series of questions designed to uncover a need or want, as well as encourage insight into a problem or need. In other words, use the Socratic method of questioning to get at the prospect's definition of value!

"Eating fried pickles was a life changing event."
- Snooki

So, as the French say: "Vive la difference!" Be a different kind of sales person. Sell the <u>right</u> value to the right prospect!

– Closing the Sale –

ACTION DRIVER ▶ *Brown Spots on the Wall*

Don't you love earning new business! Starting a new engagement with a client is exciting, exhilarating, and, yes, sometimes scary. But I relish the challenge of collaborating with a client to uncover its real needs and then craft the best solution to its problem. It's the joy of being a consultant and it's the joy of being in sales.

So, when a new prospect recently told me that his sales team didn't seem to be having fun anymore, I immediately asked how many new sales they were closing. The answer was, "Well, not as many as any of us would like." Our conversation continued while I asked many more questions and worked with the client to begin to uncover its roadblocks to closing more business. After discussing the sales team's skills, work ethic, and knowledge of and execution of the selling process, I asked about its targeted prospects: there I found one of the problems. The sales team was basically throwing the proverbial dung on the wall and hoping something would stick. You guessed it – not much was sticking.

The sales team was working with an old definition of "prospect" and working under the assumption that the market's needs had not changed. They were wrong.

Brick Wall Breakthrough

When your team isn't closing enough new business, start by looking at your prospects and asking these questions:

- Do your prospects and customers still need your services as much as they used to?
- Should you reconfigure your product line or your pricing to meet market changes?
- Is there an unserved niche that you can capture with some tweaking of your current offerings?
- Is it time to consider morphing into a new business model?

To answer these questions, ask your current customers and your prospects this question:

> "If we were your perfect supplier/partner, how would we be different from the way we are today?"

This one simple yet powerful question can focus your sales team on the prospects who need and want your offerings. The answer to this critical question can also lead to a much needed transformation. Start offering what your customers want today. Same old is just that – same old!

– Closing The Sale –

ACTION DRIVER ▶ *Johnny Gets A New Bike*

When they really want something, kids can be scrappy! A child's sales pitch goes something like this:

Johnny: "Daddy, I want a new bike!"

Father: "You already have a bike."

Johnny: "Yes, but it's not good enough. The chain keeps coming off."

Father: "Well, let's go get the chain fixed."

Johnny: "We've already gotten it fixed three times and Mr. Fix-It said he couldn't guarantee it would stay fixed."

Father: "Well, I don't know. I'll have to think about it"

Johnny: "Why do you need to think about it Daddy?"

Father: "Well, I need to think about how much it will cost and how to pay for it and how to keep the chain working so it won't cost us a lot more money."

Johnny: "If I can earn some money to help pay for it and I can learn to take care of it by fixing the chain myself, can I buy a new bike?"

Father: "Yes. If you can do all of those things, then you can buy a new bike."

Johnny: "How much money do I need to earn?"

Father: "Oh, maybe $50 dollars"

Johnny: "So if I can earn $50 and learn to fix the chain myself, I can get a new bike?"

Brick Wall Breakthrough

Father: "Yes, that's right."

Johnny: "So, I can buy the bike just as soon as I earn some money and learn to fix the chain, right?"

Father: "Yes."

With verbal agreement in hand, Johnny gets a job helping the next-door neighbor clean out his garage and he convinces Mr. Fix-It to teach him how to repair a broken chain. He has earned the right to buy a new bike and proudly purchases a shiny blue one. Three weeks later:

Johnny: "Daddy, I need a better seat for my bike!"

And so the sales process begins again.

Not bad for a twelve-year-old. When Johnny reacts this way, he understands that selling is a process of gaining agreement and, perhaps most important, it's also a **process of progressively gaining greater commitment from the buyer**. The earnest young sales kid in this example got Daddy to agree to buy a new bike. He then got his father to agree on just how much money he needed to earn, and then he next got Dad to agree to a time frame.

And – drum roll please – three weeks later this same sales whiz-kid goes after an agreement to purchase a better bike seat. Why can't all our sales people be as effective as this twelve-year-old? Perhaps it's because many of them have forgotten that **selling is a progression of gaining agreement**.

Adult sales people carry psychological baggage that gets in their way. Unlike our brave young Johnny, adults allow the fear of getting a "no" prevent them from asking for the sale. If sales people understood that there are levels of agreement they should seek before, during, and after the total sale, this fear would diminish and their success rate would increase.

Progressively gaining agreement from your customer requires persistence and fear acts against persistence. The boy in the conversation exhibited real persistence – he wanted that bike badly enough to not give up, even when challenged by objections. To repeat: he understood that levels of agreement and overcoming objections can be opportunities to success.

In the progression of gaining agreements from prospective buyers, the sales process thus includes getting prospects to:

1. Accept your call

2. Schedule a meeting

3. Share their business challenges

4. Understand the value of your solution

5. Define the urgency to act

6. Buy your solution

7. Implement your solution

8. Refer and advocate for you in other departments in the company

9. Buy more

Brick Wall Breakthrough

Yet, too many sales people approach selling as if there is only one agreement – the agreement to buy. When they fail to understand the progression of gaining agreement, they go for broke and end up with nothing, never understanding why they didn't obtain the final agreement, i.e. **the sale**.

Sales people must understand and practice three agreement elements:

1. Always know exactly what agreement you want and have a back-up agreement.

2. Identify the interim agreements necessary to earn the overall agreement.

3. Never forget that consistently asking for additional agreements is key to long-term relationships.

Defining an agreement goal insures that sales reps set the stage for getting to the specific agreement and plan for the interim agreements necessary to gain that specific agreement. In Johnny's story, he instinctively knew that in order to win the big prize agreement of a new bike, he had to get his father to agree to a series of interim conditions such as earning money, learning to fix the chain, etc.

He also knew he needed to consistently and repeatedly ask for each agreement: "So I can buy the bike just as soon as I earn some money and learn to fix the chain, right?" By asking this question, Johnny thereby set up an agreement on a time frame for purchase.

And finally, after the Johnny has made his first purchase, he goes back for a new agreement, this time on another purchase, a new bike seat – the equivalent of up-selling! Johnny was not afraid to want more and to ask for it.

But adult sales people are different, often afraid to go back and ask for more. The fear of appearing too aggressive or too greedy often prevents them from asking for more early on in a relationship.

The most effective sales people clearly understand that selling is a process of progressively gaining agreement, building this notion into all of their customer conversations. Thus they seek to:

- Commit to a specific agreement
- Establish the interim agreements necessary to achieve the overall agreement
- Secure the next meeting
- Set a time frame
- Advocate to specified others in the organization
- Consider a possibility
- Create an alternative "fall back" agreement

Genuinely understanding the progression of gaining agreement keeps a sales person from giving up. Realizing that she should always have an alternative agreement in mind is critical to keeping the prospect moving forward.

So, it may be time to learn an important sales lesson from our kids! Teach your sales reps to map (mentally and/or physically) the gaining agreement process for their next prospect or customer meeting. Each interaction will have a unique set of agreements that can be reached. Practicing the process will close more sales and will shorten your sales cycle.

And, here's to our kids – the world's greatest sales reps!

– Closing the Sale –

ACTION DRIVER ▶ *The Closing Opportunity Ladder*

As stated earlier, closing a sale is the result of gaining multiple agreements throughout the overall sales process. Sales people are naturally concerned with and focused on their selling process, but the buyer is focused on his *decision process*. A buyer's decision process can be as simple as one person saying "Yes!" or as intricate as a multiple-voiced, progressively-tiered decision.

Understanding the basic decision process is critical to knowing what agreements to seek and when to ask for them. A basic decision process might include the following considerations:

- Recognition of need.
- Assessment of purchase options.
- Resolving objections or concerns.
- Executing the product or service.

Your buyers have both rational and emotional needs that must be met at each step in the buying process if you are going to be successful in securing the agreements necessary to close the deal. The graph below details the decision process and the rational and emotional questions buyers ask themselves before making a decision.

The Closing Opportunity Ladder©

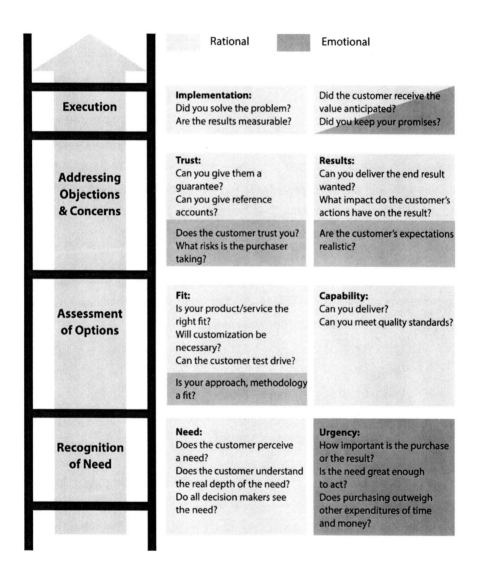

Rational   Emotional

Execution

Implementation:	Did the customer receive the value anticipated?
Did you solve the problem?	
Are the results measurable?	Did you keep your promises?

Addressing Objections & Concerns

Trust:	Results:
Can you give them a guarantee?	Can you deliver the end result wanted?
Can you give reference accounts?	What impact do the customer's actions have on the result?
Does the customer trust you?	Are the customer's expectations realistic?
What risks is the purchaser taking?	

Assessment of Options

Fit:	Capability:
Is your product/service the right fit?	Can you deliver?
Will customization be necessary?	Can you meet quality standards?
Can the customer test drive?	
Is your approach, methodology a fit?	

Recognition of Need

Need:	Urgency:
Does the customer perceive a need?	How important is the purchase or the result?
Does the customer understand the real depth of the need?	Is the need great enough to act?
Do all decision makers see the need?	Does purchasing outweigh other expenditures of time and money?

– Flat or Declining Revenue –

ACTION DRIVER ▶ *Quick! Name Two Things that Should Never Be Flat!*

OK – so the first thing that should never be flat is anatomical. What's the second thing? Your revenue of course.

Your sales team is working really hard, chasing every lead, making lots of customer presentations, but sales continue to be flat. You can't work any harder, yet revenue isn't growing and you can't seem to get at the real problem. You're not alone and finding the right answer can feel maddeningly impossible. That's because the truth is: there is no <u>one</u> answer.

Solving the problem of flat sales requires taking an honest and hard look at your company and its management. The answer will usually not be found in the easy excuses: the economy is down; there are new competitors in the market; or (my personal favorite) "We need to replace the sales team."

In way too many business situations in which sales are flat the answer instead lies in the very definition of "flat." According to *Webster's Dictionary* there are nineteen different definitions of *flat,* and there can be just as many definitions of flat sales. Two of *Webster's* nineteen are particularly relevant to flat sales:

- Having little or no sparkle (or taste)
- Having little or no interest

Ask yourself if the sales team, your marketing team, and your management team still exhibit the same enthusiasm and energy they did when sales were growing. Has that lack of energy filtered throughout the company and right down to your customers? When you do this tough self-examination, do you see:

- Tired products or services?
- Re-formulated marketing with little real sparkle or energy?
- Maxed-out, tired, bored sales reps?
- Re-energized competitors?
- Customers who no longer turn to you as the industry expert?
- Customers who have stopped saying how great and innovative you are?
- Uninspired management?

Look first at your products and services. How do they stack up against improvements or advancements in your industry? Do they meet the needs of a marketplace that changes almost overnight, or have you merely repackaged old products in an attempt to look current? Get out there and get in touch with the market all over again. What's the buzz at conferences, in industry trade journals? What are your competitors doing that you're not? Are there new features or enhanced services you must add to get that edge back? What are the new trends coming out of university research centers and/or business schools?

Once you identify what's tired about your products and where you need to update or reinvent them, move to the next stage: re-energizing your marketing efforts. In this case, don't be pennywise and pound foolish by short-changing your marketing and PR budget. If you're going to get back into the game and lead, you need "charismatic" marketing that will show people you're on top, i.e., marketing that convinces customers and prospects once again that the energy is back! Complacent marketing departments that ignore new design trends, new delivery technology, or that just plain don't see the excitement themselves, must re-energize themselves in order to spread new energy to your market.

When your products, services, and marketing are tired, so are your sales reps. No one can continue to sell lackluster products or services every day without physically leaving the company or intellectually leaving it by going into "auto-pilot" mode. Sales reps may look like they're working hard and may still be asking the customer the right needs-analysis questions, but your product may no longer solve that need. Or maybe now it's only a partial solution of the need. Despite the old Eskimo-and-ice selling metaphor, no one buys what they don't need. Flat sales can be the first indication that the need for your product is waning.

While your company was snoozing, and its life getting sucked out of it, your competitors were likely watching and cheering. While your company became complacent, they got themselves energized, they redefined their market, and, as a result, they surely stole business that would have been yours. So, watching out for the new kids on the block should never draw your attention away from that long-time competitor who may be gearing up to clean your clock.

How do you begin to put the excitement back into the company? How do you not only become relevant again but essential to your customers? This is the easy part – you ask them! If any of the problems described so far apply to your company, it's because you've lost touch with your customers. **Just ask them** and they'll tell you what they want. **Listen** and they'll tell you how to sell to them. Your customers know what's relevant to their needs and how you can reinvent your products to meet those new needs.

Focus every aspect of your company on your customers, from people to processes to technology. When you truly communicate with your customers and focus on them, they don't let you become complacent, tired, or bored again. They'll force you to stay nimble and to change with them. Try calling your top ten customers and the last ten prospects you didn't close. Ask them why they buy from you, why they didn't buy from you, and what you should be doing to earn their future business. THEN DO IT! Once you institute their recommendations, tell your customers or prospects about the important role they played in your reinvention. Thank them for saving your keister!

And finally, give your management team a kick in that keister and get them moving again by involving them actively in the process of reconnecting with your customers. Assign each member of the management team three clients to speak to. Prep your managers to ask customers how their respective departments can better serve them. Set up "innovation/ brain storming" sessions with your management team and all corresponding teams that service your top clients. Go off-site, bare your soul, ask for forgiveness for forgetting your customers. Then encourage them to lead you back to relevance!

– Flat or Declining Revenue –

ACTION DRIVER ▶ *That's Not Butter You're Churning*

You're convinced that the sales department is talented, skilled, and effective, and there've been no cuts in the marketing or advertising budgets. Your company's products and services have been around a long time and have earned a reputation for delivering value. So why is revenue not growing?

When you talk to your team and review your financials, it's staring you in the face – the company seems to be suffering from "customer churn." You're losing customers at a higher rate than you're gaining new ones. The net result is that you have to work harder just to maintain current sales levels. You're running in place!

Now that you know that customer attrition is a big part of your stagnant revenue, you can solve it by taking an honest, hard look at your company and its management. But beware! You will not find the answer in the normal excuses: the market is down, the sales people need to work harder, or (my favorite) "But we're still profitable!"

You will find the answer in an honest evaluation of the four key customer value determinants:

1. Products and/or Services

2. Sales Representatives

3. Management

4. Service Quality

But before you begin digging into the value determinants, it's wise to step back and begin by carefully examining the current state of your customer base.

Start with a Situational Assessment

Just what is the situation? It's not as simple as "We lost 50 more customers than we gained." You need to examine the data and find the story behind them. Ask questions that will expose where the customer defection is occurring. The solution starts with the right questions:

- Is the defection among all customers?
- Are you losing more long-term customers or is the defection coming from relatively new customers?
- Is the defection largest in a particular customer industry?
- Does one product line or service represent a disproportionate percentage of the lost customers?
- Is one territory losing more customers than others?
- Is one sales rep responsible for large numbers of lost customers?
- Which competitor seems to be stealing your customers? Are there trends in the timing of the losses? Is it seasonal?

Calculate average churn throughout your company based on specific factors and then compare each product, territory, customer industry, and sales rep to that average. When examining your competitors, make sure to have real data to back up your findings: anecdotal information from sales reps is not always accurate.

Powerful forces will push for a quick resolution – after all, revenue is king! But resist quick fixes. Truly lasting and effective solutions are the result of careful, thoughtful, and non-political self examination. Your fix will only be as good as the definition of your problem. The worst course is to rush to a conclusion, develop a response, and throw money at implementation, only to see revenue stay flat or, even worse, decline.

Value Determinants

The answer to customer churn will be multifaceted but will always come down to one key business differentiator: the value you offer and deliver to your customers. Your customers consciously or un-consciously evaluate several factors when making their value determination. Your self-examination should include an exploration of the same four key customer value determinants:

- Products and/or Services
- Sales Representatives
- Management
- Service Quality

Products and/or Services

The first value determinant should be an examination of your products and services. Losing customers is often due to old and tired products or services. Among other questions, answer these:

- Have your products and services remained relevant in the face of technical improvements and advances in your industry?
- Are your products and services really delivering new value, or are they merely being repackaged in an attempt to look current?

Reconnect with your market: what's the news at conferences or in industry journals? What are the new trends and technologies coming out of universities? What are your competitors doing that you are not? Are there new features or enhanced services you must add to get that edge back? In an effort to be "feature rich," have you made your products, services, or pricing too complex? Do customers really want those features?

Sales Representatives

Your sales team has a strong influence on how customers perceive your company and its offerings. Your sales reps are a key value determinant. Are they motivated? Or deflated? If your products, services, and/or marketing are tired, so are your sales reps: no one can sell lackluster products.

You should consider your sales and service team as the "voice of your customer." Making it easy for your customer to do business with you starts with making it easy for your sales team to support the customer. Internal systems should be built or re-engineered to make meeting the customers' needs paramount, and in a time frame that keeps the customer happy. Discard any of those negative assumptions about your sales team – they may not be whining. Good sales reps will know what your customers need, so ask them and involve the sales team in defining value, the same way you directly involve your customers in defining value.

Take a close look at the leadership of the sales team. Your sales team should have seen the customer churn problem coming and asked for help. Are your sales managers isolating themselves from the customer? When was the last time your sales manager received training and professional development? Are reps drowning in paperwork and meetings with little time left for coaching and client communication?

Management

Management malaise is both a symptom and a cause of customer churn. Your company's internal and external values are established by the actions of your management team. Give your management team – and yourself – a kick in the rear and get moving again by actively reconnecting with your customers. An out-of-touch management team results in an out-of-touch company.

Set up innovation or brainstorming sessions with your management team and all corresponding teams that serve your customer. Add a customer voice metric to the company plans and include rewards such as customer retention and customer satisfaction metrics. Include customer communication plans as part of performance reviews. Challenge your managers to get out in the field with customers!

Service Quality

Value is the first reason customers buy. Your product or service must answer a business need in order to be purchased. And yes, your sales rep is part of that value. But once the customer has made the decision to buy, it is *service quality* that will make her glad she chose you and it is service quality that will determine her future satisfaction. All things being equal between your value and your competitor's value, it is service quality that will differentiate you from the pack.

Brick Wall Breakthrough

As a senior manager, your role in reducing customer churn and increasing revenue is to make a sincere commitment to building a customer-driven culture that delivers differentiated service every day, in every customer interaction, from front end to back office. Successful customer-driven companies have these characteristics in common:

- Committed senior leadership
- Service as a business metric
- Commitment and active participation of first level supervisors
- Strong, consistent customer focus
- Alignment between employee and company goals
- Unequivocal commitment to continuous improvement
- Belief in and practice of employee empowerment

Flat or declining sales and vanishing customers should be incentive enough to act and make the wholesale changes you need to get your company back on track. But, just in case you need further incentive, remember that while your company is snoozing and losing its spark, your competitors are likely watching and cheering. While your company became complacent, they energized and reinvented them-selves and as a result they stole business that could have and should have been yours.

– Flat or Declining Revenue –

ACTION DRIVER ▶ *It's the Sales Team's Fault!*

Let's face it: our economy is a roller coaster with ups, downs, rapid turns, and fear as its byproduct. Too often management's response to declining or flat revenue is: "Tell the sales team to stop complaining and get to work! They need to work harder. We need revenue growth not constriction!" I ask you, just how effective is this directive in reversing a downward revenue trend?

What sales people take away from that message is, despite their previous success and dedicated efforts to exceed their goals, they were somehow asleep at the wheel, and if now they would only work harder, all will be right with the world. Faulty logic at best. Telling the team to work harder is merely counterproductive. Your best and brightest will take offense and the slackers… well, they're slackers for a reason and management proclamations won't make a silk purse out of a sow's ear.

Okay; you're saying, "I just don't get it! What 'management' means is that the sales team needs to work smarter not just harder." Well, I'll grant that there is some truth to the idea of working *smarter*. Management's role in working smarter, however, is a critical, often overlooked component. Sales teams are only as good as the tools they have at their disposal. If revenue is down, stop the blame game and take a hard look at the foundation of your selling process. Look for ways to provide support and assistance to the sales team. Take action on:

Value: Are you delivering the value customers want? Has the changing economy changed what your customer's need? Take a hard look at what you believe your product or service does for your customers, then ask the tough question: Do our customers still care?

Target: Are you targeting the right customers? The old "throw it on the wall" approach will produce revenue in good times, but it is a recipe for disaster in tough times. Working smarter starts with the right value for the right customers.

Clone Success: You will always see sales success regardless of the economy. Analyze that success. It may not simply be due to a "better" sales person. Is the success due to the territory? The sales person's vertical market? Was the success in current accounts or with new accounts? What did those customers buy and why? Build a model of your successful customers, then clone it in the territories of the entire sales team.

Lead Generation: A changing economic environment is likely to change your target customers. Examine where and how you generate leads. Assess this environment's ability to present the right value and capture the interest of the right customers.
Technology: Maximize your team's efficiency by utilizing new tech tools for lead generation, social networking, and client alerts.

Your sales team is ultimately responsible for driving revenue. But, in difficult economic times, it needs all the help it can get. **Just telling the**

sales team to work harder or to work smarter is not the answer. Give them better guidance, improved tools, and reward the right behavior.

And, should you really have some slackers on your team, jettison them as fast as you can. If they couldn't cut it in good times, there is no reason to believe they are suddenly going to "get it" and produce in tough times. Sales teams are only as good as we make them: give them the tools, the support, and the incentives to continue to succeed.

– Flat or Declining Revenue –

ACTION DRIVER ▶ *Shaken Not Stirred*

James Bond knew a great martini when he drank one. What makes a great martini is a bartender who gets the liquor proportions correct – if he's off a percentage or two then the martini is... well, not a martini.

The right proportions apply to your customer base as well. You've heard it hundreds, maybe thousands, of times: 80% of your revenue is generated by just 20% of your clients. By now you know this old axiom applies to many areas of business, but it's particularly true in sales. In today's aggressively competitive environment however, I suggest a new rule of thumb should be that if 50% of your business comes from less than 30% of your clients, an alarm should go off! You need to expand your client base and think about how you market your services.

If this new rule applies to your company, you need to quickly grow your client base by attracting new clients. But, before you send the sales team off with orders to sell, sell, sell, you need a customer acquisition model that will attract the right customers. It takes time and valuable "deep dives" to win new business, so why not seek and close the clients that will become long-term customers because they derive the most value from your services.

Brick Wall Breakthrough

Let's explore a process that will **uncover your best clients** and serve as the foundation for attracting new ones.

Identify Your Current Dependencies

Begin by examining your current clients and determining your revenue metrics. Does the 80/20 or the 50/30 rule apply? Identify the clients that generate the bulk of your business and be sure that those relationships are strong and thriving. You can't take these clients for granted while you make a shift in your strategy away from dependency. Talk to these clients often, service them to the hilt, and be sure they are receiving *real* value from you. This is the "CYA" part of the process.

Expand Your Revenue Base by Replicating High-Value Clients

Attracting, closing, and servicing new clients takes time and money, so your sales strategy and focus had better be on the right clients.

How do you define the "right" clients for your specific business? It's more than just ranking by revenue or by margin. While those vectors qualifiers are important and may be your starting point, the definition of your best target prospects includes more than just the financial factors. Understanding who your best prospects are is a process of *iterative evaluation* which, at its conclusion, will result in a clear set of client characteristics which, in turn, become the definition of your best new business targets. Identify your top 15 to 20 revenue-generating clients, then begin the evaluation process below to uncover which of their characteristics are seen in your best prospects.

Step #1: Rank by Value: Rank each of these clients by their value to your company by examining the following three factors:

- Margin Contribution
- Growth Potential
- Strategic/Value Fit

Here margin contribution is more important than revenue because the client is already a high revenue generator per its status in your top 15 to 20 customers. At this point highest margin wins.

Next, assess and rank these clients by their growth potential. Honestly ask yourself and your sales team, "Is this a client that will grow, and if so, by how much and over what period of time? Will it want the new services/products we plan to deliver? Has she bought or will she continue to buy services that "marry" her to us and make it difficult to move to a competitor? What does the long- term financial picture of the client look like? Is the client's management team focused on long-term or short-term value?" These clients' growth potential should be viewed from a 3-, 5-, and 10-year prospective.

Your *value clients* are those that benefit most from your services or products and have a strong strategic, cultural, and value fit with your company. If your services/products are designed to enhance a client's short-term value but the company is taking a long-term view, your strategic match is not strong. If you've built your company on a "high touch" high service model and your client is selling on price with service to his customers as an afterthought, how much value does your client place on your high-level service? When you raise prices, will this customer value your service quality enough to offset the price increase or will it run to the lowest cost provider because that's what its customers do? Are your cultures compatible? Long-term client partnerships are achieved because you both honor and reward the same values.

Brick Wall Breakthrough

Step #2: Look for Common Characteristics: Now let's look at the common characteristics of your top-ranking clients based on their "value" determination. Start by identifying and listing client characteristics such as:

- Industry
- Number of employees
- Revenue
- Product complexity
- Customer profile (B2B, B2C, demographics)
- Market position
- Market reputation

You're looking for commonalities that could point to future prospects. If all of your clients sell complex products, your strategy might be to market only to companies with complex products. Uncovering similarities helps in creating compelling success stories that will resonate with prospects and shorten your sales cycle. Understanding these similarities can speed sales training and product development.

Step #3: Gauging Your Value to Your Client: What products or services are these high-value customers buying from you? Can you develop a list of recurring and similar problems you are solving for these clients? What business problems do your clients solve for their clients? How does your service help them do that? Within your client's organization, who buys from you? Do you know why they buy from you?

For the real answers to most of these critical questions, **ask your clients**! Talk to the clients who rose to the top as a result of this process. Ask them why your company is important to their success and then ask for referrals to companies they think match your newly-identified target prospects.

Realigning Your Sales Strategy and Sales Force

By honestly and carefully using this process to really understand your best customers, you are now in a position to expand your customer base by targeting and closing the <u>right</u> clients, not just any client. It's time to realign your sales and marketing strategy to focus on these prospects and to realign your sales reps so they can effectively prospect and close based on this new set of client characteristics. Do you need to switch from territories to industry verticals? Does your sales team need training of any kind in order to act as "business consultants" to the newly-defined target client? Does your compensation structure need updating in order to reward and encourage a new prospect focus?

You should perform the 50/30 rule analysis annually to gauge your progress at moving beyond just a few clients. This analysis will also serve as your early warning system. If the metrics are good and if your dependency has been eliminated and is not degrading over time - good for you! But regardless of your progress away from dependency, you should perform the complete analysis at least every three years to be sure that the ideal client characteristics have not changed. If they have, you'll have the data needed to drive strategic change in your sales and marketing.

– The Sales Environment –

ACTION DRIVER ▶ *The Chicken or the Egg?*

Does your sales management reflect the style and culture of the organization, or is the style a reflection of your sales manager? Does your sales team reflect the style of your manager, or is your sales manager's style the reflection of your sales team? The answer to both questions is: Yes!

And there's the conundrum. Which comes first depends on your company's understanding and acknowledgement of the fact that style plays a huge role in how you sell, as well as – according to some experts – how much you sell. But regardless of the real beginning, your sales manager will absolutely define the type of sales people you hire, reward, and retain, so you need to be sure you have or are recruiting the right sales manager.

Let's start at the real beginning: the product or service you sell. What you sell determines <u>how</u> you sell, and how you sell should determine the configuration of your sales staff which, in turn, determines the management style you should hire.

Still confused? Let's examine two fictitious companies:

- Company A sells precision tools that are, well, precise. When manufactured, the specs are detailed and unchangeable. Company A is not in the custom business – it's in the precision replication business. The price charged is hugely influenced by the cost of materials and, with foreign competition, Company A's margins are narrow. The market is clearly-defined and possibly limited, and the skill of A's sales force is not a deciding factor in making the sale; it is the quality, precision, and price of the product that sells.

- Company B, on the other hand, sells technical education, such as network training. The content of the training must be customized to the needs of Company B's clients and may need to cover multiple geographies. The price is determined by the value add brought to the table, as well as by the skill of the sales team and technical instructors.

Should the sale forces for these companies have the same skills and talents? No. Company B needs sales people who are flexible, creative, and independent, reps that can think and adapt on their feet. It needs to craft high-value-driven solutions that pair the right content and instructor with the right client, all while building in value added extras to keep margins up and protect the company's enormous investment in ever-changing equipment and continual staff education. Company A needs a sales force that is process-oriented, price-focused; one that adheres to strict company policies and procedures in order to insure compliance and product quality.

The products these companies sell determine the what type and style of sales team they require. In turn, the sales team style determines which management style the team needs to achieve the best results.

There are three main styles of sales management: **Commander**, **Director**, and **Leader**. When recruiting, it is vital to your sales success that you hire the style that supports the way your sales team needs to sell.

Commander

This style is built on process, policies, and careful monitoring of your sales team. The *commander sales manager* knows at all times how many cold calls, appointments, and proposals were made by her team that week. This style focuses on the activities, actions, and hours for which the sales staff is responsible. Revenue generation is important, but what is more so to this sales manager is not the end result but "how I got there." Reports are numerous and detailed, and failure to complete such reports is a clear negative. Performance reviews are often based on the behaviors, attitudes, and skills that the Commander believes are important, rather than on objective metrics.

Director

The *Director* sets a course, defines the end result, and then lets his team find its way to success. The Director's staff is expected to act independently, protect the margins, and effectively balance the sometimes conflicting needs of the customer with those of the company. Field and activity reports are minimal. The Director can tell what and how you're doing by the revenue metrics you deliver. Support, coaching, and territory direction are minimal. Goals are clear, but the road map may be sketchy or even absent. Performance reviews are based on end results such as profit margin, margin contribution, and market share. Total revenue dollars are just the first layer of evaluation.

Brick Wall Breakthrough

Leader

Balancing staff independence with the need for consistent messaging, service promises, and brand identity, the *Leader* blends the best of both the other styles. She learns to adjust her management methods to the needs of the individual sales person and build sales teams that reflect the product or services they will sell. Leaders strive to hire talented, creative, committed sales professionals who require minimal super-vision but appreciate road maps and managerial support. Leaders encourage independence and are not afraid of reining in the lone rangers who can sometimes result from that independence.

As you can see, the product or service your company sells defines the sales management style you need to build the best sales team for your unique product and market characteristics. In the fictitious companies above, a Commander would be most logical for the precision tool manufacturer, Company A, as she would build and retain a sales force that desires clear direction and for whom independence is not a priority. Company B, whose product requires creativity, decision-making strength, and independence, would be best served by a Director. A Leader sales management style would thrive and be happy at Company B as well, but she would likely not be as happy or as successful at Company A.

Sales management style matters because it sets the direction and the character of your sales force. Determining the style that will give your sales team the highest level of success begins with examining your products or services and letting them set your sales direction, thus setting your recruiting guidelines for sales managers.

But a word of caution! Your company may have become comfortable with the current sales management style despite its mismatch to your product. For instance, the company's culture may not support an independent sales force if previous managers were Commanders. The company may be accustomed to detailed reports and the security – however false – those reports engender. Examine your company culture for its appropriateness to the required sales management style. You may have more work to do than just hiring the right sales manager!

Determining the Most Effective Sales Management Style

Company Characteristics	Commander	Director	Leader
The skills and knowledge of the sales person have a major influence on the close of the sale.		X	X
The sale is more influenced by price.	X		
The product is not customizable.	X		
The sale is heavily dependent on problem solving.		X	X
Being the customer's "trusted advisor" is highly desirable.			X
Sales staff is inexperienced.	X	X	
Sales staff is experienced and knowledgeable about the industry.		X	X
Multiple buyers are involved in majority of sales.			X
Government or industry regulations are critical.	X		X
The product is a commodity.	X		
The sales are complex with a long selling cycle.			X

– The Sales Environment –

Is It Time for a Cape and Mask?

Bravery is the Key to Selling in Tough Times

Recession/no recession, depression/no depression: confused? Worried about the future? The economic up and down is very likely to be a way of life for a while.

In the face of tough times is it important to **be brave, stop worrying, and take ACTION**! Under difficult economic conditions, too many businesses seek cover, crawl into a ball, and wait it out. Wrong move! Want some advice? OK, maybe you don't, but here it is anyway: think beyond survive; **think thrive**. If you take the right actions you can thrive! Think superhero! Be brave and go where no man has... well, you get the picture.

Here are seven actions you can take to increase revenue even in a recession:

1. **Aggressively market and sell.** Attack each day with renewed energy. Ignore your tendency to want to pull back on marketing. This is the time to examine your marketing; jettison those tired old messages and market aggressively. Energize your staff

and your customers by marketing with new creativity and confidence. Look at new marketing avenues and absolutely increase your networking. Don't let salespeople "hunker down" and get lazy because they think no one is buying. Someone is always buying and it better be from you!

2. **Connect with prospects, current customers, and past customers.** Up sell to current customers. Re-ignite relationships with past customers and give them a reason to come back. They're worried about a recession too and buying from someone they know can be reassuring. Create new incentives to keep your sales team selling. Look for new ways to get leads. Create short-term bonuses that will drive your sales team out of the office. Consider paying for "nos." The more nos your sales reps get, the more calls they've made and the higher your chances of landing new business.

3. **Train your sales team and transform your processes.** Training can sharpen skills and energize your staff. Training doesn't have to be a big investment. Create "buying groups" with other companies – fill the training classes together and save money. Purchase leading sales books, read them as a team, and discuss them in your sales meetings. In addition, transform your processes by making it easier for customers to buy from you and for you. Make it easier to deliver superior service. Transforming your people and your processes will deliver results.

4. **Innovate, invent, and identify.** Create new products or services that will demonstrate increased value to your customers both old and new. Resist the temptation to say, "We'll hold off on development because nobody's buying." When you innovate, tell

the world through your website, PR, direct mail, and letters from the president. Your new service or product could be the key to new sales. And, most importantly, identify with your customers. What do you have that can help them through a recession? Ask your customers what you can do to help their businesses grow? Give 'em more, not less. Not only will this bring in revenue now, but it will build strong relationships that will reap benefits for years to come.

5. **Opportunities abound; seize them.** Be opportunistic and look for new markets, new partners, and new networks; move out of your comfort zone. Create an Advisory Board to give you ideas and guidance, now and for the future. Look for synergy with other businesses and create opportunities to cross sell.

6. **No retreat, no surrender!** Never let 'em see you sweat! It takes courage to lead a company in an economic downturn. If you want your staff to sell and your customers to buy, you need to model confidence and excitement. Taking calculated risks and being brave is contagious - you can keep your staff confident and your customers buying by showing them what innovative, motivating leadership really is!

7. **Take action throughout the company.** Fight the fear and the belief that "protecting" your business is the best you can do in a recession. Remember: "He who hesitates is lost," and that is never truer than in a recession. Be bold, be brave, and lead the charge for new business.

– The Sales Environment –

ACTION DRIVER ▶ *Will That Be Paper or Plastic?*

Turn on the TV, log onto the Internet, or read a newspaper, book, or magazine and you'll hear how you and your company can "go green." *Going green* means taking actions focused on protecting our environment and our natural resources. Regardless of how you feel about the movement, few people disagree with the concept of safeguarding the environment.

As I sat on a plane headed for "the green paradise" of Florida, it occurred to me that the green principles of reducing pollution and waste, recycling, and protecting our resources apply to our sales environment just as readily as they do to our physical environment. A healthy sales environment is the foundation for profitability. Here are some actions you should take to protect your sales environment:

- **Reduce the Sales Pollution.** Is your sales environment being polluted by negative, derogatory comments about the competition? About management? About difficult customers? About the "other sales people who don't pull their weight?" When your sales team is presenting to prospects or clients, do you hear the same old story? Are they emitting hot air and failing to sell the value you offer? Time to clean up the environment by focusing on the positive. Capture new client success stories, refocus the team on your customers and their needs, and conduct an unbiased audit of your competitors, one that reminds your team that denigrating the competition only makes the team, not the competition, look weak.

- **Reduce Waste in Your Processes.** Seriously examine each step in your sales process and compare it to your customers' buying processes. Are they in sync? Where can you eliminate non-value-add activities? Where can you add value for your customers? Can you trash the paperwork that adds more frustration than value for your internal and external customers? Do you really know which marketing efforts have a clear ROI? Look for waste everywhere, then get rid of it.

- **Repeat Business, Don't Recycle Business.** Recycling and counting on the same old customers is easy – too easy. That false sense of security is the weak link your competitors will capitalize on to steal your business. You must earn repeat business by consistently providing new value, higher levels of service, and consistently talking to and listening to your customers.

- **Your People are Your Business, so Protect Your Resources.** Surprised when one of your best sales people leaves the company? It's a wake up call you should heed. Keep your best people happy by regularly rewarding them with money, training, recognition, and new products to sell. Review your compensation plan annually to insure that it reflects changes in the market and in employment opportunities. Examine territories annually for distribution fairness. Freshen and update marketing materials and sales tools. And, fire those non-performers. Nothing demoralizes good sales people as fast as ignoring the slackers!

Perhaps the most important aspect of the green movement is the acknowledgment that man and his environment must be in balance. In the business world, the most successful companies acknowledge and act on the same premise: that their customers are partners, and that in any partnership both parties must receive equal value.

When this "value scale" is unbalanced, you place short-term goals over long-term ones. You are happy with quick sales due to manipulation rather than an open, honest dialog with your customer or prospect; you choose fast-to-market over product quality. Just as the green movement attempts to secure a healthy physical future, adapting these principles to your business environment will insure a long, healthy future for your company. Time to go green in your sales environment!

– The Sales Environment –

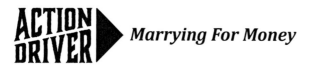 *Marrying For Money*

Have you sat in a room where Sales and Marketing have each tried to throw the other under the bus? Sales blames Marketing for terrible leads, while Marketing blames Sales for its inability to convert leads into business. It's never a comfortable scene.

The marriage between Sales and Marketing is typically arranged and often loveless. But if these two parties cannot put their egos aside and work together for the good of the business, then revenue will suffer.

The Marketing–Sales Relationship

To achieve business success, it's critical for Sales and Marketing to understand and respect each other's unique roles, as well as the challenges each department faces.

Here are three things your business can start doing today to achieve a stronger link between Sales and Marketing and, as a result, enjoy more revenue:

1. **Clarify the responsibilities of each group**. Marketing is responsible for bringing qualified leads to the door. Sales is charged with closing these leads. Each group must own its responsibili-

ties and do all it can to execute them successfully. For example, if a sales person feels her presentation skills are weak, it's her job to improve them. If a marketing manager feels his materials are not as compelling as they could be, it's his job to enhance them. Clarifying roles will prevent the spillover effect in which each department begins to tell the other how to do its job.

2. **Establish a continuous feedback loop between the two groups.** Sales must share how sales conversations are going, what objections it's facing, and which types of leads are converting most successfully. Marketing must share information on the materials it's developing, messages it's communicating, and any adjustments it's making. And, Marketing should seek input from Sales before calling the collateral or online content "written in stone."

3. **Take a big picture view at least quarterly.** Taking a step back to discuss "bigger picture" issues, i.e., industry trends, competitors, and new products or services that could help their efforts, can help forge relationships between Sales and Marketing. Because these meetings are not focused on specific marketing materials or the conversion of specific leads, the blame game can be put aside and everyone can think about the company as a whole.

Sales and Marketing must remember that theirs is a marriage driven by the need to generate money, and they must ignore the "arranged" aspect of their relationship.

– The Sales Environment –

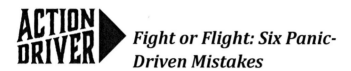 *Fight or Flight: Six Panic-Driven Mistakes*

It's a difficult selling environment today! Hell, it's always a difficult selling environment! In the face of real challenges, too many sales reps are making critical mistakes that cost them and your company money.

As managers, we need to recognize that our sales teams face a choice every day: stay and "fight" through the tough times, or take "flight" emotionally and/or physically. Controlling the responses to this challenge is especially important for companies whose products often have high price tags or are within marketplaces where a need must be created for new and innovative products and services. You need to watch for panic-driven mistakes and act fast to address them, while supporting your sales people emotionally.

Mistake #1: Nobody's Buying. If you haven't heard this saying, you're either very lucky or deaf. This kind of verbal negativity can be so debilitating it causes sales reps to shut down, to just go through the motions. In the face of reduced budgets, these reps can fail to demonstrate that your product or service will increase efficiencies and produce results. In other words, they forget to sell the ROI that can create a budget where none existed.

The Answer: Share every sales success story no matter how small. Invite a customer to a sales meeting to talk to the team about why he bought from you, what value the purchase brought to his company, and how his company has benefited.

Mistake #2: Failing to Qualify Leads. Many sales reps fall into the trap of believing that any lead is a good lead. They are so desperate for a "live one" that they waste time and energy following bad leads.

The Answer: Give your team the permission to <u>not</u> chase every lead. Instead of asking, "What are you going to do to sell this guy," ask your sales reps what they have done to *qualify* the lead and why they believe it is a qualified lead.

Mistake #3: Shortening the Discovery Phase, Moving Too Quickly to Product Presentation. Panicked salespeople often try to get to the product presentation quickly in order to ask for the close quickly. But this approach may cause them to miss the customer's real needs and the cues that reveal how to customize their pitch to a specific customer need.

The Answer: Stop conducting "What did you do this week?" sales meetings and turn them into training opportunities. Remind everyone that there's a sales process for a reason and ignoring or diminishing a step in the process will not close more business. Demonstrate that discovery itself is a process of "gaining agreement" and of leading a customer to acknowledge a problem for which you have the solution.

Mistake #4: Failing to Adjust to the New Reality/Failing to Change. Certain aspects of selling never change, but how you do it does. Repeating what you have always done before may not work now. Challenging economic environments should push you to examine every aspect of your sales process, your product, and your marketing.

> *The Answer:* How one presents its product or service is definitely going to be different over time. Prospects can be afraid, so products or services should be presented in a way that alleviates or eliminates fear as much as possible. Change the context in which you present your product or service. Describe the benefits and results in fresh terms that matter to the prospect.

Mistake #5: Failing to Respond Appropriately to a Slower Customer Decision-Making Process. Decisions are taking longer. We need to adjust to that new reality and build strategies for it. Calling or emailing the prospect constantly will not force a faster decision.

> *The Answer:* Accept that in a slow economy your prospects are likely going to think and rethink every purchase. Be damn sure you can clearly and effectively state your value proposition in specific terms relevant to your buyer. Influence the buying criteria and the decision process. Stay in front of the prospect by adding value during the decision-making process, such as through offering a free trial or seminar.

Mistake #6: Failing to Ask for Help. In our culture, asking for help can be viewed as a sign of weakness. But you can't help your team if it doesn't ask.

The Answer: Create a positive environment that encourages coaching and mentoring among peers. In private one-on-one meetings, ask salespeople how you can help them. Avoid group discussions that require them to come "out of the closet" about their fears.

This list is by no means comprehensive; many other mistakes can happen over the course of a business's life. But it is management's responsibility to see them coming and prevent them. Above all, management needs to keep a watchful eye for signs that panic-driven mistakes are occurring, then act swiftly to conquer them.

– The Sales Environment –

 *To The Moon Alice!*

We elect a President of the United States every four years. A U.S. senator is elected every six years – with a third of that body changing biannually along with our entire House of Representatives. Add all our local, state, and city elections, and we pretty much have an election going on all the time. I try to be an informed citizen and watch the debates, but the only thing I become more certain of is that these politicians' claims of accomplishment or failure become more ludicrous with each passing race. And as each candidate tries to outdo the other with new and innovative ideas, we citizens end up with suggestions as far-fetched as "Let's colonize the moon!"

Should we ever, in fact, colonize the moon, I'll trade all of my worldly goods to select the first ten people to go – honestly, all my worldly possessions!

Histrionics aside, the political debates – especially presidential ones – remind me of the sales process. The sales process requires the introduction of an idea or solution and the discussion of the reasons behind why that particular solution is the right one for the prospect or client. Success in both sales and politics is tied to how well you listen to your prospect's needs and wants, and how effectively – and, **most importantly, how truthfully** – you position your product or service. In this vein, the sales call can be considered a debate between the sales person and the prospect.

Ask yourself these questions about your sales reps:

- How closely do they resemble politicians when they talk to prospects?
- Are they truthful when presenting your services and capabilities?
- Can they conduct a debate with a prospect about your product without defaming your competition or exaggerating the results your product or service can deliver?
- Can they effectively solve objections?
- Do they believe that the ends justify the means?

The answers to the above questions lie in how your sales reps' manager believes prospects and customers should be treated. Political candidates use attack ads because they work – what that says about the American public is a discussion for another day!

But does badmouthing your competition work in the long run? What does it say about you as a company? You want customers for life, not just for the next two four-year terms. Sales people who demean their competition or who sell on price alone lack confidence in your product and clearly do not understand your value proposition. Perhaps more important, they don't respect your prospects or customers!

Do you know how your sales people sell? Do you ride with them on new sales calls? Do you make the sales people practice presenting your service in front of the team? Do you role play difficult customer sales calls and coach the team through them? I don't need to tell you that the answer should be "Yes!"

Establishing colonies on the moon may or may not be feasible, advisable, or reasonable, but without a valid need for doing it and a thoughtful plan to execute the idea, it sounds… well, you know what it sounds like. Selling is no different. Your sales people must first and foremost establish that the prospect has a need for your product, then demonstrate that they have the right solution. Just making wild claims doesn't earn trust, whether in politics or selling!

– The Sales Environment –

ACTION DRIVER ▶ *Please Sir, I Want Some More*

Oliver Twist uttered that phrase when he wanted more gruel for his one daily meal at the orphanage. You can bet that, in Dickens's day, such a request was met with a resounding NO. As a sales executive, not an orphanage caretaker, you know that sales incentive compensation plans should provide the financial rewards necessary to motivate sales professionals to take the initiative, apply the energy, and deploy their skills to transform a prospect into a buyer.

You also know that too many sales compensation plans fail to meet that goal. They fail due to questionable quotas, overly-complex formulas, poor tracking mechanisms, and misalignment with the company's strategy.

So how <u>do</u> you develop effective sales incentive compensation plans? Follow this Five-Step Cheat Sheet!

Step #1: Define the Strategic Mission. Your company's strategy must drive both the design of the plan and the key performance indicators measured by it. Therefore, to establish both your strategy and your performance indicators, ask yourself such questions as:

- What is the marketing vision for the company?
- Are you opening new markets or introducing new products?

- Are you in a mature market that is becoming commoditized?
- Are individual product margins good but volume too low? Or, conversely, is revenue growing every year but profits are lagging?

Step #2: Design the Plan. Keep it simple. Complex sales compensation plans frustrate your sales team and those who must manage it. However, keeping it simple requires serious work and thought. Let's now explore the biggest issues around the design phase of sales compensation plans:

- **Key Performance Indicators.** This is where sales managers go crazy and build plans that monitor and reward everything they think sales people should do. Wrong! Good sales compensation plans focus on only three performance measurements based on your strategy:

  1. *Production goals* based on revenue, margin, or units.
  2. *Sales effectiveness goals* that focus on new accounts opened, product mix, up selling, and cross selling.
  3. *Customer relationship goals* that reward account retention, customer satisfaction, and market share.

The three performance indicators you choose must also be aligned to your strategy. This is the point where most sales plans fail – they choose too many performance indicators and/or the indicators chosen do not align with and advance the company strategy.

- **Base Salary Versus Variable Component.** One of the most difficult aspects for management is deciding the percentage of base salary versus the variable component of a sales incentive compensation plan. Management always worries about overpaying on a base salary and underpaying on the variable/ incentive portion.

Before you make any decisions, ask yourself what type of sale drives your profit? Does making a sale depend upon the relationship with the customer, or does the product you sell drive sales? Would a defecting sales person take their accounts with them due to relationships, or is your product or service the real value to the customer?

Companies that sell commodities and have serious competition earn revenue due to the efforts and relationships built by their sales representatives. Knowledge-based businesses, such as consulting, earn revenue through the skills and knowledge of their consultants/ sales reps. In both cases, the customer buys from you <u>because of your sales representative</u> and will likely follow him to his next company. If this dynamic exists within your company, the variable portion of the compensation should be high; it is a reflection of the reality that your sales person drives relationships and should be rewarded accordingly.

If, however, your product has unique value, you have limited competition, or customers remain with your company despite sales rep defections, then the variable component of the compensation plan should be lower.

In general, relationship-driven sales plans should have a lower base-to-variable ratio (50/50) while product-driven companies should have ratios closer to 70/30 base-to-variable.

- **Quota Assignments.** Sales quotas and/or goals should promote active selling and energize the sales staff. Sales reps must believe that the quotas/goals are attainable. In general, you should establish quotas that you realistically believe can be reached by 60% to 70% of your team. Remember to take revenue seasonality into account when assigning quotas. Quotas begin with the sales forecast for the year and are only as realistic as the overall annual revenue forecast.

Step #3: Compensation Plan Implementation. How you handle the implementation of your compensation plan is a major factor in how your sales team will respond. Sales reps must trust the new plan. How you position, communicate, and implement the plan affects their trust level. The new plan must be documented and should include examples of how it will affect their earning potential. Quota, territory, and account assignments must be fair, equitable, and documented.

You should also develop a transition plan that addresses how the team will move from the existing plan to the new one. Will you move "cold turkey" to the new plan, or will you have "leveling guarantees" to ease the team into it? Leveling guarantees can have real benefits – retention being one of them – but you can't delay the goal of the compensation plan which is to meet company revenue/profit objectives.

Step #4: Management and Administration of the Plan. How you manage and administer the plan builds trust. Tracking and reporting results must be done frequently and accurately. The formulas and calculation methods must be transparent to sales reps.
Wherever possible, avoid paper calculations and massive spreadsheets which often confuse and frustrate sales reps. Consider purchasing Sales Incentive Management software from companies like Synygy™, Centive™, NetSuite™, or Xactly™. Remember that as compensation plans change, job descriptions and performance evaluations will also likely require

some adjusting. Managing to the plan should also include a well thought out "coaching" plan to support individuals toward success.

Step #5: Evaluation of the Plan. Building your sales incentive compensation plan is not a once-in-a-lifetime event. You should annually review the results against your strategy and expectations of the plan and make needed adjustments. Reexamine your company strategy, then start the process again. Don't make your sales team beg for more as Oliver had to. Your compensation should be fair and competitive and, above all, it should handsomely reward great performance.

– Deep Dives –

Sales

To learn more about the concepts discussed in the Sales Chapter of *Brick Wall Breakthrough*, consult these texts:

The Closer (5ᵗʰ Edition), Ben Gay, III (2004, LJR Group/Hampton Books).

Compensating the Sales Force, David J. Cichelli (2010, McGraw-Hill).

Customer Centric Selling, Michael T. Bosworth, John R. Holland (2004, McGraw-Hill).

Discover Your Sales Strengths, Benson Smith, Tony Rutigliano (2003, Business Plus).

The Five Keys to Powerful Relationship, Sallie Sherman, Joseph Sperry, Steve Vucelich (2003, McGraw-Hill).

Hope is Not A Strategy, Ted Gee (2008, Dog Ear Publishing).

Major Account Sales Strategy, Neil Rackham (1989, McGraw-Hill).

Marketing for Rainmakers, Phil Fragasso (2008, Wiley).

No More Cold Calling™, Joanne S. Black (2006, Business Plus).

Brick Wall Breakthrough

The Perfect Hire: A Tactical Guide to Developing & Retaining Top Sales Talent, Katherine Graham Leviss (2011, Entrepreneur Press).

Sales Coaching, Linda Richardson (2008, McGraw-Hill).

Sales Management, Robert Calvin (2004, McGraw-Hill).

Selling to Big Companies, Jill Konrath (2005, Kaplan).

Secrets of VITO, Think and Sell Like a CEO, Anthony Parinhello (2006, Entrepreneur Press).

The Seven Keys to Managing Strategic Accounts, Sallie Sherman (2003, McGraw-Hill).

SPIN Selling Fieldbook, Neil Rackham (1998, McGraw-Hill).

The Team Selling Solution, Steve Waterhouse (2003, McGraw-Hill)

Trust-Based Selling, Charles H. Green (2005, McGraw-Hill).

The Trusted Advisor, David Maister, Charles Green, and Robert Galford (2001, Touchstone).

CUSTOMER SERVICE

– Service Fundamentals –

ACTION DRIVER ▶ *Life's Tough, Get A Helmet!*

I was introduced to this phrase at a conference at Mt. Auburn Hospital in Cambridge, Massachusetts, where I was one of several speakers. During lunch, one of the doctors relayed a story about a recent circumcision she had performed. Just before the big moment, the baby started to whimper. The doctor immediately felt empathy for her tiny patient. His mother, on the other hand, turned toward the baby and said, "Life's tough, get a helmet!" Ouch!

I must confess to loving this statement despite the circumstance. I started thinking about all the times in business when the phrase would be appropriate. Times when, as an executive, manager, or supervisor, you have to take a stand and demand excellence.

Life's tough, get a helmet! when:

- Your sales team complains it can't sell your product because the economy is bad.
- Your customer service team bitches that it has to deal with difficult customers who aren't nice.
- Your manufacturing boss tells you that production is behind schedule because a vacation prevented regular maintenance and it has to be done now!

- The project manager informs you in a meeting that he can't meet the deadline that is two weeks away.

And on and on and on.....

But what really jumps out for me is how that phrase applies to our customers. Just what exactly do we do every day to "provide the helmet" for our customers? What actions should you be taking daily to insure your customers don't need a helmet? And when they do, that you have one ready in their size?

How do you provide protection and assurance for your customers? Ask your customers what they want and need from you. How often do you survey your customers and ask how you're doing? Better yet, when was the last time you interviewed your customers or held a focus group to learn how you stack up against your competition? How often do you check the online chatter about your company? And, most important, do you implement what you learn or just ignore those "over-demanding, unrealistic customers?"

So here are some suggestions:

- **Develop written service standards**. Have you developed written standards of service for each and every role in the company? Remember, everyone's performance, from front office and sales to production and warehouse, affects your customers. If your non-customer interfacing employees don't know or don't believe they affect customers, you have a problem that needs attention. How quickly and accurately your warehouse boxes, labels, and ships your product directly impacts your customers. How precisely your product is manufactured is definitely a quality issue that affects customers. Customer service extends throughout your company.

- **Measure those standards**. Setting standards without measuring them is worse than wasting time – it tells your employees that you really don't mean what you say. You've got to mean it, and to mean it you must measure it. Establish metrics for each service standard – everybody has telephone answering standards, right?! Time to move beyond the obvious and ask how long should it take to process a sales order? To check out someone at the register? Set specific metrics and then measure them.

- **Train your team in the standards and techniques of superior service delivery.** People cannot do what they don't know or don't know how to do. Training is vital to success, but it is not the total solution. How many times have you trained your staff members and within 90 days they revert to their old ways. That's a clear sign that management is not monitoring or coaching. Management is not holding people accountable or establishing clear consequences for inaction.

- **Create strategies to sustain customer focus**. Success is realized by companies that understand that sustaining customer focus and performance levels is the real key. What will you do three months after you've instituted standards? After training? Supervisors should discuss service at every meeting, continue service training, review customer surveys with the team, and together develop solutions.

- **Hold your team accountable for the standards.** Without accountability only truly internally-driven employees will keep up the good work. Job descriptions and performance evaluations must include your service standards and metrics. What?! You don't do formal performance evaluations?! Start NOW! It's only human to want to know how well you're doing and to want it confirmed in writing. Verbally patting someone on the back is great and should occur weekly, if not daily, but it doesn't become real until it's in writing.

Even when you follow all the above recommendations, you will fail to make every customer happy. When you fail at meeting your customer's expectations – and all businesses do – consider what you need to do to return the customer to a satisfied state? Do you have a service recovery process in place? And, most important, does your front line staff have the power, authority, knowledge, and desire to make things right for the customer right now?

What do you do when you've followed the above procedure to deliver superior service, have implemented a real service recovery process, and have managed, mentored, and coached your team, and some of your players *still* won't get on board? Give them a new helmet! Trade them to the other team and bring in a replacement! There's more than one kind of circumcision...

Hey – life's tough and so is business.

– Service Fundamentals –

ACTION DRIVER ▶ *GPS: Super Tool or Annoying Mechanical Voice?*

While driving several years ago from North Carolina to Ohio to visit a relative, I took a detour. Not an intentional detour… one of those "Geez, is that what the map meant?!" detours. Fortunately, my husband woke up in time to see a church ahead and scream, "Oh my God! How the hell did we get here?!" Here was Beckley, West Virginia, and the church was where his uncle was a pastor. Beckley was not on our route to Columbus, Ohio!

Yes, I had a map, and yes, I thought I was following it. But that's the trouble with a map. It's neither definitive nor directive. You must decide which of the many possible routes to take to reach your destination and, in my haste and in the dark, well… I chose the wrong option. My husband hailed the emergence of GPS systems in an effort to guarantee I wouldn't get us lost again.

To move faster to your goal of becoming a truly customer-driven organization, I'm going to act as your GPS and hand you the directions to your destination. First, let's discuss what it means to be *customer-driven* and not merely *customer-focused*.

Brick Wall Breakthrough

Being a customer-driven company means you:

- Build products, systems, policies, and procedures to support the **customer's** needs more than just yours.
- Deliver more than just good customer service – you deliver service that differentiates you from your competition.
- Consistently ask your customers how you're doing, then **act** on their suggestions.
- Rewrite jobs, roles, and responsibilities to include customer service standards and expectations.
- Define, measure, and evaluate service performance to insure accountability.
- Sell and market on the premise of meeting customer needs.
- Build and structure customer relationships for the long-term.

And how do you achieve service nirvana? Take the following steps:

1. **Create a Service Vision**. Your company and/or team must understand your vision and be able to "feel it" the way that you do. Everyone needs a working vision, a **mantra** to guide their every day work.

   One of best examples of this is the Ritz-Carlton Hotel Company. Its service vision was written years ago to tell employees how to act, make decisions, and service customers. Witness the Ritz Carlton service mission statement:

   The Ritz-Carlton Hotel is a place where the genuine care and comfort of our guests is our highest mission. We pledge to provide the finest personal service and facilities for our guests who will always enjoy a warm, relaxed, yet refined ambience. The Ritz-Carlton experience enlivens the senses, instills well-being, and fulfills even the unexpected wishes and needs of our guests.

Now THAT'S service! And to make it easy for its staff to remember and act upon the mission, the Ritz-Carlton created this simple service statement:

We are ladies and gentleman serving ladies and gentleman.

Powerful stuff. Your journey to service excellence begins with your vision and action statement. Take your time. Consider including customers in the creative process. Your service mission statement will become the foundation for all future actions.

2. **Clearly Define Your Customer Profile.** Draw your staff a picture of both your ideal internal customer and your ideal external customer. To define the actions you need to take, you and your staff must really "get" these ideals and build to their needs. Think of your most difficult customer and aim for perfection by creating service that will make her happy. A boss once told me, "You're only as good as your most difficult customer." Your clearly-drawn picture of the internal customer will provide guidance in hiring and promoting staff, and will reinforce the idea that superior internal service will deliver excellence to your external customer.

3. **Benchmark Your Competition**. What service level does your competition deliver? Where are they deficient? How does your industry compare to others? What can you learn from other industries? And remember, delivering the same quality service as your competitors is just an ante, merely table stakes to get

into the service game. Going beyond that bet into better quality service means that you will take the whole pot.

4. **Define Differentiated Service**. Where can you excel? What can you do better or differently than the market? Delivering differentiated service is the real goal. The Ritz-Carlton is the gold standard in service, that which other hotels attempt to emulate. You want to be the gold standard in your industry.

5. **Develop Defined, Specific Service Standards**. Each role within the company should have written service standards; not just the obvious ones like the time frame for returning phone calls or how many times the phone rings before it must be answered. I'm talking about **deep standards** that drive performance excellence. Set a standard for accuracy in billing, for proposal turn around, for problem resolution – for every department in the company.

   One of my clients wanted to improve the accuracy and quality of its shipping and packing. It created a "Know Your Packer" program in which every packer placed in his/her boxes a note with his/her picture and a request to call him/her directly if the customer noted a packing problem. Errors dropped significantly and a sense of pride in the department became prevalent. Innovative deep standards beget better workers and better service.

6. **Measure for Accountability**. Service standards should be measurable and part of everyone's performance appraisals. Accountability is a must if you are serious about achieving service superiority.

7. **Develop a Written Problem Resolution Process.** In addition to cross-department, company-wide problem resolution processes, each department should have its own internal system. As you do this, push the authority to solve a customer's problem, including financial compensation, down to the customer interfacing level. Don't make a customer have to ask for a supervisor to get a resolution. After all, what does this ultimately tell the customer about you and your company? Two things:

   - You don't hire people who are prepared or capable of truly servicing me, **and**
   - You don't trust your staff to act professionally or rationally.

   Both of these concepts are huge negatives in my book. If you're worried about the service team giving away too much of the profit to make a client happy, then set a dollar ceiling after which the problem must be escalated. Clearly define this escalation ladder, and be sure that someone who can solve the problem is <u>always</u> available.

8. **Create a Reward System.** Like any behavior you wish to create and reinforce, you need a reward system that says "damn good job!" It need not always be money: recognition goes along way. But a word of caution: never – I repeat never – create a "service employee of the month" award. After three months, these fail to garner enthusiasm and the belief that you "had" to pick somebody takes over. Rewards are most effective when they are unexpected and are given in the moment.

Brick Wall Breakthrough

So, now you have your GPS for driving the company toward service superiority. How you implement these steps will be and should be unique to your culture, your products, and your industry. You might experience detours along the way, so stay focused on the goal and allow yourself and your company occasional failure. Failure is how we learn. Though Beckley, West Virginia, wasn't on the direct route to Columbus, Ohio, I learned a few things from that detour!

– Service Fundamentals–

 *Hey – It Ain't by Accident*

So, you want to deliver great service?

Processes define customer service quality. You do all the things manage-ment is supposed to do to ensure great customer service. You've listened to your customers, defined customer service, and set service standards. You've included service delivery standards in job descriptions and per-formance evaluations. You've provided training and coaching. You have a bonus program for great service delivery. And yet, both your customers and your support staff are complaining. Why? Because you neglected the underlying truth that **processes drive service**.

Process improvement is the least sexy of the service components and is frequently messy. Effective process improvement takes time, honest self-examination, and a willingness to change. For these reasons, many organizations ignore the processes and policies that drive their service quality. Your business processes send employees the signals about how they should execute their jobs. If you're serious about delivering superior service and making service a market differentiator, it's time to examine what your processes are telling your staff and your customers.

Process improvement begins with the "voice of your customer." You can't and shouldn't attempt process improvement until you've identified the processes which directly affect your customers, and have conducted conversations with your customers about how those processes affect them.

How do you select which processes to examine and, if warranted, improve?

Your process improvement initiative should include a close review **from the customer's view point.** Processes should be designed for more than just ease of execution by your staff. It may be easy for you but detrimental to your customer. You should look at the total customer experience from beginning to end. Examine the processes that affect your customer's ability to:

- **Compare your product or service to your competitors:** Unless you're selling an inferior or overpriced product or service, don't be afraid to let your potential customers compare your offerings to your competitors. Encourage and guide them through the process. In the end you'll have a stronger sale and longer-term customers.

- **Evaluate your product or service:** Demos, case studies, testimonials, fact sheets... part of your comparison should involve a close evaluation of your product or service. Demos are wonderful tools; however, if demos are not appropriate, make it easy for the customer by sharing case studies or examples of how your product or service will work for them. Give the prospective customer testimonials of success.

- **Ask presale questions.** Most organizations have a good process that allows the prospective customer to get questions answered – they're called sales and support staff. BUT, how easy is it to reach sales or support, and how educated are they on the implementation or use of your product?

- **Purchase your product or service.** Making it easy for customers to buy your product seems like a no-brainer, but this is so often an ignored element of the customer experience. How many people must the customer interact with to complete the purchase? How many pieces of paper must he complete? Is your online process short with simple directions? If your product requires customization before the purchase is complete, how well do you guide the customer through that maze?

- **Use or deploy your product or service**. Are instructions for using the product clear and concise, or do you need a Ph.D. to get it up and running?

- **Pay for or finance your product or service**. What payment or financing terms do you offer? Are your invoices accurate? Very few things anger a customer more than inaccurate invoices – they assume you're either incompetent or dishonest, neither of which strengthens your relationship.

- **Make contacting you easy:** Don't bury your phone number in layers of pages on your website. Don't make the customer wade through voice mail hell before you tell them how to reach a live representative. The vast majority of organizations have taken automation to such extremes that the general public now feels service is dead. We all know how to yell "Representative!" over and over into the voice mail system to eventually get a human, but by the time we hear a live voice, we are already frustrated or – worse – pissed off.

- **Get problems resolved.** When the desire to improve service strikes an organization, they often begin the improvement at the end of the chain, i.e., where the customer is unhappy. While creating and maintaining the processes of handling and quickly resolving complaints is absolutely critical to service quality, take the time to build or re-engineer all of your customer interfacing processes. Your complaints will dramatically diminish and customers will have a better attitude toward the organization when and if they have problems.

Processes power the "how to" element of customer service and therefore drive employee behavior. Well-trained, customer-driven employees simply cannot overcome bad processes, especially when everyone is left to their own devices to make and keep the customer happy. Customers experience inconsistency in this relationship and managers complain of a "cowboy" mentality among their staff. Make it easy for your employees to serve your customers and make it easy for your customers to do business with you. Build and re-engineer the relevant processes to meet your customer's expectations.

– Service Fundamentals –

The Little Black Dress or Dark Business Suit

Kudos to the daring men who read past this title! No, this is not about fashion; well... maybe it is. Customer Service fashion!

What's the latest trend in customer service? Social media of course! Thousands of businesses are using social media to communicate with and track their customers. Several years ago *Investors Business Daily* ran an article citing Best Buy, Dell, and Comcast as among the leaders in effectively integrating social media and traditional call centers to "talk" to and "listen" to customers. Today, every good company has deployed social media networks as a means of staying in touch with customers.

Social media tools like Twitter, Pinterest, Facebook, and a myriad of other online tools are effective and are today's «sexy» fashion, with new options roaring onto the scene every day. But for many, the need for constant updating and tracking of these tools can be daunting, thus they may never use the them.

Maybe its time to retrieve that little black dress (or suit) from the back of the closet. Remember, they're there because they're timeless – great for cocktail parties and funerals alike. That black suit goes anywhere and so do the tried and true tools we used <u>before</u> the social media onslaught! If you've thrown up your hands and given up on communicating with your customers because navigating the technology is too challenging, think again. **You can't ignore your customers!** Dig into the closet and pull out that customer-communicating little black dress or suit.

Talking to your customers is always in style. There are still easy and highly-personal ways to talk to them. Don't ignore the more traditional yet highly-valuable tools you used a few years ago. If the high tech methods aren't the right service tools for you, then get back to basics. When was the last time you:

- Conducted a customer survey via phone, mail, or online?
- Conducted a targeted focus group?
- Hired a third party to interview your customers <u>and</u> your non-customers?
- Just asked the customer in front of you how you can better serve her?

Your customers <u>want</u> you to ask them how to build a better relationship. So ask them. If you're a retail store, try asking the customer standing in front of you to take a short four-question survey in exchange for a 10% discount coupon. Asking customers to go online for a chance to win something is <u>not</u> effective – memory fades and so does the willingness to give you their time; instead, direct your customers to your website where they can download a discount coupon upon completion of a survey.

If you're a B2B business, create that **customer advisory board** you've always wanted. Include a short survey with your first invoice, and again, in the <u>middle</u> of the engagement. Ask your customers about your brand identity, your service, your product knowledge, the results you delivered, and ask them if they'd buy from you again – then ask why or why not.

High tech communication tools are great if we use them. But don't let their complexities keep you from going back to basics in order to stay in touch with your customers. That little black dress or business suit is always fashionable and so is talking directly to your customers!

– Service Fundamentals –

 *Px6*

If asked, you'd probably admit that process improvement has been part of your strategic plan for ____ years – fill in the blank! Like many companies that embrace the concept and its value, you find that <u>implementing</u> process improvement just never seems to happen. Living in the moment, fire fighting, launching new products, or the simple dislike for such operational issues are just a few of the barriers to actually implementing a process improvement initiative. Let's face it – process improvement is not as sexy as saying you launched a new product, a new technology, or a new sales approach. It's like replacing the plumbing when what you want is a whole new bathroom.

But the time for improving the way you do business is NOW and, in changing economic climates, it's imperative! And remember the results! What business wouldn't like to:

- Reduce costs
- Improve margins
- Improve employee morale
- Improve customer relationships

Brick Wall Breakthrough

Achieve those results via the **Six Ps of Process Improvement**:

P1: Prioritize. Just as your company can't be all things to all of your customers, your process improvement initiative must be focused and discreet. Start by focusing on areas where you and your customers will reap the greatest and fastest benefits. Realizing a result quickly is especially important for your first project – save the big, complicated ones for later when your team members are experienced at such initiatives and past successes will fuel them past the inevitable rough spots. Prioritize based on saving at least one of three things: time, money, and energy.

If the process you choose to improve affects your customers in any way, seek their input in advance. Ask if the improvement would be their priority. Ask what value, if any, improving the process will have for them. If what you want to address is not ranked highly by your customers, consider choosing another process to work on.

P2: Purpose. Clearly define the purpose, i.e., the **desired outcome**, of the process improvement initiative. What metrics will illustrate success? Can you track the savings you anticipate? Do you have existing metrics against which you can compare the project results? Securing buy-in from your team and company rests on a clear, definable, and agreed upon purpose and goal.

P3: Process Project Charter. The improvement team should create a Process Project Charter that defines:

- Purpose, goals, and success metrics
- Project team member roles and responsibilities
- Levels of decision-making authority
- Stakeholders: internal and external

- Project management plan and timelines
- Reporting and meeting frequency

The charter should be the guide for the project. It will insure consistency, reduce competing agendas, drive accountability, and encourage transparency throughout the project.

P4: People. It could be argued that managing people is the most critical success factor in process improvement projects. Process improvement begins with selecting the right people for the Process Leadership Team. While it is important to have team representatives from the departments and divisions that will implement improvement, who you select is vital. Ignore titles! Team members must be leaders, but titles don't necessarily signify real leadership. Select people with positive can-do attitudes. You want people who ask, "Why not?" backed by analytical members who will contribute the careful examination necessary to turn innovation into reality.

And don't overlook the contributions your customers can and should make to the effort. Seek their input before, during, and after the initiative.

P5: Prove. Over 30 years of marriage to a scientist and over 20 years of running companies has tempered my "Just do it!" personality. Risk-taking is admirable when you consider improvement options and developing new products, but it can be disastrous if you roll out a new process without testing it first. Nothing works right the first time – if you've ever assembled toys at Christmas, you know that the brightest and the best still need practice. Test your new process! Running a redundant process for a short period may increase work load, but it will absolutely prevent disaster. Explain to your customers that you are testing a new procedure for a short period and would like their input and patience. Advance warnings that things may be different will prevent surprises, and no one likes surprises less than your customers!

P6: Profit. Let's face it, we're in business to make a profit and you need to know how the improvement project contributes to your bottom line. Did the initiative reduce costs? Increase your margins? Speed a new product to market, or in other ways contribute to the bottom line? Some process improvement projects don't possess characteristics that can be directly traced to the bottom line, but they must have measurable results! If the goal was to improve customer relationships, then the "how" must be measurable. If the goal was to save time, then the "how much" must be measurable.

The most successful improvement projects also create a plan for capitalizing on the improvement. What future rewards can you reap as a result of the improvement? What actions can you take to achieve that future reward? Will you be able to earn new business? Will your sales cycle time be reduced? Can you reap new business from existing accounts? Tracking the anticipated rewards will provide ammunition and incentive to create a continuous improvement environment, seen by many as the Holy Grail of business!

Improving how your company does business through process improvement is a concrete method of improving margins and reducing costs. It improves competitiveness without the cost of new products or reduced pricing. It enhances your customer relationships, which lead to an increase in revenue per account. It adds value to your customers which should improve margins through higher, more value-focused pricing. It attracts new business and enhances your quality reputation. The beauty of this approach to contributing to your bottom line is that is it entirely up to you! You drive the results, not the marketplace.

– Service Fundamentals –

ACTION DRIVER ▶ *No Damn It! I Need It Now!*

In conducting interviews with customers for a new client, we heard our client's customers say repeatedly, "[They] have no sense of urgency. When you raise a concern or problem, you never know when or if you're going to get a resolution. Getting an order confirmation could take several days."

If you haven't yet figured out that customers "want it now, damn it," then you've been living in a cave. As a customer yourself, you know you want your needs met right away. Why then, when we become managers or service deliverers, do we forget that fundamental truth? Why do we forget that what we want as customers is exactly what our customers want?

Have you ordered anything off the Web recently? Sure you have, and within seconds of placing your order, your order confirmation appears in your email box. How's that for fast? The Internet has taught your customers to expect speed – and damn fast speed at that.

How fast is your company at:

- Delivering product or services?
- Confirming orders or returns?
- Processing orders?

Brick Wall Breakthrough

- Building a product or designing a service?
- Resolving customer complaints or problems?
- Returning phone calls or answering emails?
- Thanking customers?

If you don't know the answers to the above service factors, or more importantly, if you don't have metrics to monitor and measure your speed and quality, then its time to get cracking and insure your team is proactive, fast, and empowered to meet your customer's needs.

If you sell a product, do you maintain enough inventory to serve your customers, or do they have to wait for you to restock? If you sell a product that's used in conjunction with another product, do you proactively inform your customer when you make a change to your production? Do you give them time to recertify your product as a part in theirs?

Even if your business is not product-driven, such as a service business, you still have service metrics to monitor. For instance, during the above customer interview process, my colleagues and I provided weekly updates to our client that included a list of completed interviews, next week's scheduled interviews, and a list of its interview prospects who had not responded. Based on the project's progress, we updated the completion date each week. We anticipated our client's need to know and made sure he didn't have to ask us!

> "We call it **infectious impatience**. That's the hallmark and we are trying to inculcate it in the entire organization. Infectious impatience. So that things not only get done, but get done in double quick time."
> - Mukesh Ambani
> Business Tycoon

Your revenue is dependent upon repeat business and repeat business is dependent upon service quality. Anticipate your customer's needs! Manage their expectations! ACT NOW! Don't give your customer a reason to think about getting answers from your competitors.

– Service Fundamentals –

 *He Said/She Said*

Your sales team tells clients that the new product will be released in three months and that next month they'll get all its specifications, a full two months before this information is released to the public. Clients are thrilled to beat the competition by getting advance information.

Your customer service team tells callers, any and all, that the new product information will be available in 60 days. Your marketing department has just updated your website to include the details and specs of the new product release in an effort to prime the market.

Sound familiar? It should! These misrepresented service promises are made to customers every day by many organizations, maybe even yours too!

During an exercise on Service Promises which was part of training we delivered to the Home Health Care division of a non-profit organization, the group discovered that its website had just posted an explanation of a new service it was planning to offer – the operative word being "planning." "Oh my God!" were the director's exact words when she reviewed the website as part of the exercise. "We haven't even worked out the process for delivering this yet – I need to take a break right now and talk to marketing!" A frightening but true story.

The Service Promise

Your clients are receiving information every day telling them what to expect from your organization. These expectations are your *Service Promises*. Regardless of whether you consciously create, define, and/or communicate these service promises, they determine exactly how satisfied or dissatisfied your customers are and will be with your company. Disconnects in service expectations occur every day, unless you have put the following things in place:

- A clear definition of your Service Promise
- An understanding of the role service plays in your organization
- An organization-wide commitment to service, led by senior management
- Clear communication across all functional departments within your organization regarding your company's service standards
- Assigned responsibility for service within your organization

The Role of Service: Brand, Promise, or Luck?

"We're Job One!"
"The Customer is our Business!"
"The Customer Comes First!"

These are all well-known branding statements built around the belief that differentiated customer service drives profits. And these statements are right, *if and only if* these promises are kept.

Most businesses today claim to be committed to the customer and make service a high priority. Many go so far as to make service statements like those above in order to differentiate their brand. Your company may not have chosen to use service as a branding component, but I'd bet that service is "talked about" and emphasized enough that your staff has gotten the message that "we need to promise great customer service."

Your staff may be making service promises every day in response to management comments. Here's an example of how an executive can talk about service one day in a speech, only to see it translated into a promise that the staff then carries directly to the customers:

> The senior management of one of our clients recently attended an internal sales meeting and talked about management's efforts to work with suppliers to reduce the number of back orders and to fulfill them within 30 days. The next day, sales people began "promising" customers that they'd get their back-ordered items within 30 days. Even though the issue of back orders had not been totally or officially resolved, the intent quickly became a promise – a promise that the company was not ready to keep.

If you make such promises, they must be kept or customers will eventually move to your competition. In some organizations, meeting the customer's service needs and expectations is a matter of luck more than strategy. Such organizations simply got lucky in hiring employees who were naturally dedicated to serving others. Such luck, however, doesn't last and these companies invariably come in last in their industry. But if you have chosen to make service a part of your brand, or you have at least made service promises to your customers, you must keep those promises if you want to stay in business!

Here are some basic steps you can take that will improve your odds of keeping your service promises:

- Create a "Service Leadership" team of representatives from senior management, operations, product development, marketing, sales, and finance.
- Define your company's Service Promise and incorporate it as part of the organization's mission and vision statements.
- Define and distribute specific service standards for each department.
- Train the entire company in those standards and how to deliver superior service.
- Develop a formal "Service Recovery System" and monitor failures for process improvement.
- Define and assign the responsibility for monitoring your service promises.
- Develop an ongoing service improvement methodology.

Keeping Promises Protects and Increases Your Bottom Line

Committing to delivering high levels of service that truly drive your bottom line is difficult and requires real discipline. If your company is willing to make a long-term commitment to the hard work of delivering differentiated service, you should begin by developing a service quality program that includes the key elements of service quality improvement: define, measure, innovate, train, and sustain. Here are the key steps:

- **Define** your service promises and standards and build those standards into job descriptions
- **Measure** your success at meeting those standards and include service performance in performance evaluations
- **Innovate** by continuously improving and refining your service
- **Train** the entire company and develop on-going programs that will keep the company focused on service

- **Sustain** the enthusiasm for increased customer satisfaction by broadcasting the effects of service initiatives and rewarding those employees who exceed your standards

Most importantly, **listen to your customers**. They will tell you what they expect and how you can meet those expectations. Delivering differentiated service is not an event; it's a journey that starts with keeping your service promises today.

– Service Fundamentals –

 *Pinky Swear*

*Focusing on customer retention tactics, such as service
recovery and reducing customer defections by just 5% through
service, can boost profits by 25 to 125%.*

This quote is from a 1990 *Harvard Business Review* article by Frederick F.
Reichheld and W. Earl Sasser, Jr. These statistics pushed businesses to take
a hard look at the quality of service they delivered. The realization that
businesses needed to focus on service quality was made strikingly clear.

Now, more than 20 years later, it is not enough to just deliver good service
– your competitors are also focusing on service. Today it takes <u>superior</u>
service delivery and recovery to reduce customer loss and thus increase
profits. While truly becoming *customer-driven* takes time and serious
commitment, there are things you can do today to build customer retention – you can keep your service promises!

How? By first determining what promises you are making:

Promises by Your Employees: What are your employees promising
your customers in the sales cycle, in delivery, or in service recovery?
Are your employees setting the right expectations for your customers? Are your sales people so eager to close the sale that they tell

customers special order items will arrive in two weeks even though they know it will take at least four? Are your consultants guaranteeing an unrealistic revenue growth percentage to get the sale? Does your delivery department give a realistic delivery date and time, or does it cave in and tell the customer what they want to hear? You need to know whether a disconnect exists between your employees' words and reality.

Online Promises: What does your website say to customers? Does it mislead customers through promises of "overnight" delivery which, to you, means starting two days after their order gets out of the warehouse? Has marketing jumped the gun and announced a new product or service on the website before your sales and service teams have been trained on the new product? Do you know who is tweeting on behalf of the company and what promises she may be making? How about your blog?

Universal Promises: Product Development excitedly tells Sales about the pipeline of new products that are "almost ready" and Sales immediately starts promoting the product. Your return policy says: "Bring it Back, No Flack," but your return paperwork is onerous for customers and employees alike.

Keeping your service promises means:

- **Managing your customers' expectations.** Making promises you know you can keep. Never over-promise, just over-deliver.
- **Managing both implied and stated service promises**, regardless of where, how, or by whom they are made.
- **Fixing the promises when they are broken**. Push authority to solve problems to the front line. Clearly state and insure that all

employees know the solution to your biggest challenges. Make it easy for customers to complain and follow up when they do.

Gather your staff and ask them what promises they've made to customers over the last 48 hours. Assess the validity of those promises. Ask the staff to review every piece of marketing, every contract template, all invoices, your website pages, blogs, Twitter, Facebook – scour any place where your company name appears for promises, then evaluate what you have to do to make good on them.

Don't make promises you can't or don't want to keep just because they sound good. Someone will hold you to it. Better to make fewer promises and keep them!

– Service Fundamentals –

 *The Bronze Rule*

Have you ever overheard a child turn an old axiom on its head and redefine it in the context of their environment? At age six, when confronted with a nasty playmate, my best friend and I would "give her back her nasty," which usually included making faces and verbal taunts. This *quid pro quo* turned the Golden Rule into "do unto them as they do unto you." My mother named this the "Bronze Rule" due to its ability to tarnish those who gave back the negativity they got. The stress in today's workplaces is making the Bronze Rule all too evident in customer service these days.

I experienced the Bronze Rule recently when I tried to call the telephone company to question the bill for our cottage in Maine. The bill had consistently gone up over three months despite the cottage being closed and the phone locked in the shed. After waiting 18.6 minutes (yes I timed it) to get someone on the line, I was told that the company's files were not available and had not been for three weeks due to problems with the transfer of the files from the old telephone company. "No, I don't know when they'll be available," was the response I received when I asked when they could examine my bill and give me an explanation. Pick your jaw up off the floor – this is not an exaggeration! The telephone company could not access my bill!

Brick Wall Breakthrough

As a customer service consultant, I felt compelled to ask the customer service rep (CSR) if she was having a bad day. "Bad day! Lady, the new company laid off half the old staff, didn't plan for how they were going to convert systems, and they cut my hours." Guess who really felt the shaft that the company gave their employees – their customers! This customer service rep gave her customers what she got from her employer – frustration and disrespect!

In tough economic times you may take tough action to cut costs, and layoffs may be one of those options. BUT... you need to consider the ramifications of those actions on your customers.

Here are some things you can do to protect your service quality despite staff reductions:

- Restate the company's focus on delivering great customer service
- Restate your service standards to **everyone**
- Talk to your staff about why the layoffs are necessary
- Work with the remaining staff to develop a "service plan" in light of the loss of resources
- Prioritize customer needs and focus on those that are most important to your customers
- Create a service award program, or if you have one, add a new award to encourage and reward great service (e.g., the Service Purple Heart, the Service Medal of Honor, etc.)
- Talk openly about organizational and individual stress and ways to cope with it.
- Randomly select customers to call bi-monthly to ask about your service and how you can improve it

You can't afford to lose a single customer! Lapses in service will drive away existing customers, tarnish your reputation, and make it twice as hard to earn new customers now and in the future when the financial world improves. **Replace the Bronze Rule with the Golden Rule!** Customer Service is and should be a competitive advantage!

P.S. Despite my superhuman powers, I couldn't crawl through telephone lines and slap that customer service rep upside the head – believe me, I TRIED! Instead, I slapped her company by filing a complaint with the Public Utilities Commission of Maine. Your customers will also take such actions; worse, they'll go to your competitors!

– Service Fundamentals –

 *What? Me Sell? NEVER!*

When the economy becomes your enemy in selling your products or services, **selling your value** becomes more important. I train my sales staff to talk about the company's real value to a customer or prospect. We pay marketing firms to come up with catchy value statements and then we insert them into all the company's marketing stuff, from the website to Facebook to old fashioned printed material.

But are Sales and Marketing the only departments that should be selling your value? Don't overlook the ability of your CSRs to sell value. I'm not talking about cross-selling or up-selling – that's focused on new products or services that increase revenue. **I'm talking about the value that builds customer loyalty and creates long term revenue from customers for life.**

Customer A has just called your customer service team to complain that your product has stopped working and he needs someone to fix it NOW!!! Your CSR says:

> *I can understand how you must feel. I will send a field technician to your site within two hours. I'll follow up at 4 p.m. to be sure the problem is fixed. Will this solution work for you?*

Brick Wall Breakthrough

This is a great conversation. The CSR acknowledges the customer's frustration, gives him a specific time frame for the fix, offers to follow up, and involves the customer in the solution by asking if it works for him. But is something missing? The customer doesn't know that two hours is a terrific turn around time, nor do they know why you can respond so quickly. So, let's try that conversation again:

> *I can understand how you must feel. Because we keep our service territories small, I can have a field technician to your site in two hours. The smaller territory allows us to service faster than most other companies and we know that higher level of service is important to you. I'll follow up at 4 p.m. to be sure the problem is fixed. Will this solution work for you?*

By sharing why smaller territory has value to the customer, the CSR has just positioned the company above its competition and cemented the customer relationship.

If your CSRs aren't clearly reinforcing all those built-in, value-added qualities, you're missing a unique opportunity to build customer loyalty (*n.b.*, if the CSR is working from an office overseas, you can count on them not introducing your value). Reinforcing your worth when a customer is unhappy is more meaningful to her because your value becomes more than just marketing hype. Your customers can see literally and figuratively why your company is the best partner for them.

Here are a few suggested service rep statements that can add value:

- **Large Inventory**
  "Because we maintain a $2 million dollar, 10,000-part inventory, we can have a technician with your part to your

site by the end of the day and have you up and running immediately."

- **Recent Training**

  "That 's a really tough problem; but because our technicians receive quarterly training, they are knowledgeable in the up-to-the-minute solutions. Steve will be there in three hours to fix the machine."

- **Customization**

  "We've maintained a 30-year relationship with ACME and, as an exclusive Gold Partner, our team receives higher level training on your equipment. We'll be able to customize the equipment to your specific needs so you don't have to send the equipment to ACME."

- **Industry Specialization**

  "Tax law is very complicated Mr. White. But we have an entire team that specializes in only tax law and it will be very happy to guide you through the maze. When the firm was founded, we realized that no one person can know everything so, to give our clients the highest level of service and knowledge, we chose to specialize."

These examples are intended to get you thinking about the unique value you deliver. Not sure what that value is? Don't turn to the marketing guy – he'll come up with platitudes. **Ask your customers what they value most.** Then get your employees to brainstorm a list of why they believe you are different than the competition. Get real. Remember that value is in the eye of the beholder. It is only valuable to your customer if it furthers his personal goals or the goals of his company.

Brick Wall Breakthrough

After communicating with your customers, take their value answers and develop statements for each of them. Your CSRs can use these statements when talking to all customers. Turn a service call or customer problem into an action that drives loyalty.

– Customer Loyalty –

ACTION DRIVER ▶ *Mom Likes Me Best!*

My brother and I are very close in age and grew up almost like twins. But, sibling rivalry was always there despite our staunch defense of each other to outsiders. When we were really mad at each other and wanted to inflict pain, one of us would yell, "Mommy likes me best! She always gives me the biggest piece!" It didn't matter if it was a piece of cake, pizza, or meat – what mattered was that it was the biggest!

This example of "more equal than others" came to mind when talking with a client about its desire to create named levels of service, such as "platinum," "gold," and "silver." This approach starts out with the desire to offer Platinum Customers a higher level of service, but often morphs  into new pricing strategies that require the customer to pay more for the services they used to receive for being... well... a great customer.

Tiering customers is common and born from the desire to build strong, resilient relationships with top revenue-producing customers, an important goal when achieved for the right reasons with the right actions.

Brick Wall Breakthrough

But delivering different levels of customer service to stratified levels of customers is a slippery slope. Customer favoritism is risky. There are serious dangers in defining customer service levels by revenue tiers:

1. You open the door for your service staff to decide that certain customers are not "worthy" of their time or extra effort. Don't delude yourself into thinking that your "well-trained, dedicated, and highly-rewarded" service team won't write off a lower-tier customer as unworthy. At the first sign of serious customer anger, the unworthy customer will suffer.

2. You give your service staff a ready excuse for not performing at their best all the time. "He's a Silver Customer; just tell him the warranty's expired," becomes an acceptable response to a customer's genuine problem.

3. You reduce your opportunity to use superior service as way to turn customers into Platinum Customers – it's the old chicken and the egg conundrum. "They don't get the service until they become Platinum!" But remember you got the first Platinum Customers by exceeding their expectations.

4. You risk losing your Silver and Gold Customers to the competition who are eager to turn them into their Platinum Partners.

Delivering superior service should be the mission of your staff every day, with every customer, without fail! Building lasting relationships with customers is critical, but there are other ways that are more productive and tie you and your customer together – mutual success is a powerful driver.

Nurture your top revenue producing customers by **building a relationship based on mutual success**! Encourage – no <u>require</u> – your sales team and your service team to really get to know your key customers. Understand how your product furthers your customers' goals and, most importantly, how it affects their relationships with their customers.

Instead of defining your service delivery by the worthiness of your customers, consider strategies for creating and sustaining lifetime customers:

- **Solve customers' problems.** Take the time to use your internal expertise in systems, channel development, or recruiting and work with them on their problems.
- **Anticipate customer needs**; don't wait to be asked. Go to them with ideas and solutions.
- **Partner for innovation**. Collaborate with select customers on developing new products or services, yours and theirs. Again, mutual gain is a powerful driver.
- **Create a formal, official communication strategy** between you and the customer that is more than asking the sales people to "stay on top of things." Unless you build a reward system for this relationship strategy, your sales team will be focused on new business. Just staying on top translates into only being there when the customer wants to buy again.
- **Invite customer participation in your strategy sessions**. Seek their input – but be sure to act. Don't ask if you don't intend to act on their feedback.
- **Create a "Customer Advisory Board"** with rotating membership that regularly solicits ideas about how you can better service your customers.

Brick Wall Breakthrough

When you create synergistic relationships based on mutual need and mutual success, you are building strong, lasting relationships that will drive and increase your revenue – because it drives and increases your customer's revenue! In the valid desire to nurture your top customers, don't lose sight of the fact that superior service is the foundation for every customer relationship and should never be used as a tool to reward or punish customers.

– Customer Loyalty –

ACTION DRIVER ▶ *Surprise, Surprise!*

From our first surprise birthday party to a surprise marriage proposal, we learn that surprises are fun! Surprises are special because by definition they are unexpected. Delighting our customers and delivering differentiated service takes more than great people and consistently meeting service standards and processes. It takes the unexpected.

Giving your customers "positive surprises" creates buzz about your business and creates a bond with your customer. Positive surprises build customer loyalty. When the answer to why you did something special is a simple "just because," it has power! So what can you do to give a customer a positive surprise? Here are a few examples:

- A furniture company delivers a new bedroom set and in one of the drawers is a thank you note and a lavender sachet to scent the drawer.
- An appliance store delivers and installs new kitchen appliances and inside the refrigerator is a thank you note with a coupon for groceries.
- On the anniversary date of the account opening, a bank sends a silver half dollar and a thank you note from the president expressing gratitude for your patronage.

Brick Wall Breakthrough

- A health insurance broker sends a customer a discount coupon for an hour-long, stress-relieving massage.

Be creative! Have fun! But be unexpected. Sending cards or gifts on holidays or renewal anniversaries is not unexpected and is obviously self-serving. Create your own holiday, partner with another company – like the local grocery store or a newly-established massage therapist – and everyone benefits. Build customer loyalty by doing something "just because!"

– Customer Loyalty –

 *Lock 'Em Up and Throw Away the Key*

I bet you'd like to lock up some of your customers and throw away the key! But we both know that's impractical, if not impossible.

Unless of course you're the only provider in the world of what they need. Boy, wouldn't that be fantastic?! Instead, you may be watching helplessly as your hard-earned customers walk out the door before you've up-sold, cross-sold, or renewed them for another year. Would you objectively describe your customer relationships in terms of "churn and burn"? If the answer is "yes," then you don't need me to tell you that you're working too hard to lose money. What you do need to do is make drastic changes in how you conduct business – and fast.

There are many reasons why companies experience high turnover in their customer base year after year, but there is one fundamental solution – turn your focus from inward to outward. Companies with high customer turnover rates are not focused on serving their customers in every aspect of their business. Your customers' needs must be paramount to how you sell, how you deliver products or services, how you resolve problems, and, most important, how you determine and deliver value to them.

Brick Wall Breakthrough

First speak with those customers you have lost; ask them what you could and should have done differently to earn their long-term business. Then talk to your current customers and ask them why they bought from you and what they will need from you in the future. Listen to them.

Take what you learn and make it the foundation for a true commitment and consistent focus on four aspects of your business:

1. Effective sales professionals and systems

2. Differentiated customer service

3. Continuous business process improvement

4. The creation and preservation of a culture that embraces change and exhibits flexibility

Excellence in each of these aspects is what drives sustainable, profitable relationships. Can you build longer-term customer relationships without demonstrating superior performance in these areas? Yes! Companies do it every day, but their number of long-term customers is shorter and profit margins on each are lower. We're talking about creating the kind of relationships that keep competitors at bay and the margin-per-customer climbing year after year.

Maximum Sales Effectiveness

Maximum effectiveness in sales requires the right people and the appropriate support systems. Your sales professionals must be customer-driven and service-oriented, and they must excel at consultative selling. They must also be skilled at listening, conducting good customer-needs analyses, and, above all, problem solving. As "visionaries," your sales team will help your customers learn how to build their businesses and will recognize unique up-selling and cross-selling opportunities that come along in doing so. Your sales team should be able to identify opportunities to build partnerships and alliances that will further the goals of both your customers and your company. In short, your sales reps must become trusted advisors with a defined strategy for account management.

Sustaining highly-profitable customers depends on your ability to give them significant value beyond the inherent positives in the product or service you are selling. Adding value dictates that your sales team is working at the highest levels within the organization. Through business analysis with senior management, you will learn about these customers' business goals and strategies. Further, adding value means that your sales professionals must offer the knowledge that enables your clients to make better decisions which, in turn, will enhance their business capabilities. Sales professionals, in short, must be lifelong learners, gathering knowledge every day that can be transferred to your customers.

Differentiated Customer Service

"Differentiated" customer service is not necessarily the same as "great" or "superior" service. Instead, *differentiated service* is that which truly sets you apart from the competition. Your competitors – at least the good ones – are all working to deliver "great" service because the market expects it. But sustainable customer relationships are the result of a true "service culture" that is visible to your customers through your sales team and the ease of doing business with you.

Thus, a differentiated service culture is built on customer-driven service standards throughout the company, not just the front-line staff. It is built upon a commitment to service measurements and service-performance management processes. With formal systems and training in place, a truly customer-driven organization insures that differen-tiated service is delivered every day. This organization has a formal, structured service-recovery system that tracks the problem, solves the problem, and institutionalizes the correction. Long-term customer relationships are next to impossible to build in a competitive market without consistent service that starts at superior service and matures into <u>differentiated</u> service.

Continuous Process Improvement

Don't panic. When I say "continuous process improvement" I'm not talking about re-engineering the whole company or throwing out what works. What <u>is</u> necessary is to examine the processes that directly affect your customers and determine where they can be streamlined, improved, or even eliminated. The goal here is to make it easy for your customers to do business with you by developing a consistent, company-wide methodology for examining processes, especially via communicating the improvement process and implementing corrections. Remember, a process cannot be improved in isolation. You will rarely find a process that is singular to one department.

Embracing Change

Finally, your organization must exhibit a culture that embraces and survives change. In the past, change was linear; you could make plans to deal with changes one at a time, as they arose, while employees and managers had at least some time to adjust and adapt to the changes.

But in today's business environment, changes take place <u>across</u> the organization simultaneously, and they are increasingly driven by customers.

Simply listening to your customers will prompt change within a customer service organization, but once your company has transitioned to an organization that is truly customer-driven, this change will become dynamic. The commitment to deliver differentiated service both internally and externally will become second nature to the entire organization.

– Customer Loyalty –

Boxers or Briefs: How Well Do You Know Your Customers?

Do you define success by the length of your client list? Are you content with low margins per account? Does high customer turnover make your day?

I didn't think so. Despite the obvious undesirability of these account characteristics, you may still suffer from one or all of them. So the question becomes how to create profitable customer relationships that then turn into long-term customers?

The answer to retaining customers is found in superior account management. Knowing your customer so well that the question of "boxers or briefs" is irrelevant – because you already know the answer.

Building sustainable, profitable customer relationships is the result of "customer intimacy." Customer intimacy comes from two-way interaction and a deep level of mutual trust between your company and your customer. Developing this trust takes time. Earning your position as a customer's "trusted advisor" is the outcome of effective account management and, most importantly, adding value above and beyond the inherent value of your product or service.

Brick Wall Breakthrough

Strategic Account Management

Account management is "strategic," not "tactical." You're not managing the details as much as you are managing the structure, direction, and outcomes of the relationship. The goals of **Strategic Account Management** are to:

- Add maximum value to clients based on their value perceptions
- Allow for the greatest opportunities for knowledge transfer
- Build close contact with decision-makers throughout the customer organization
- Create opportunities for mutual learning and feedback
- Increase revenue and profit margins by doing all of the above!

When these goals have been realized, you will have developed a sustainable and more profitable customer relationship. You will realize the benefits of increased profitability, longer-term relationships, and protection against competitors; and you will gain knowledge that will help you improve not only your business, but that of your customers.

Adding Value Through Knowledge Transfer

We have all been told time and time again that we live in a knowledge-based economy. Knowledge is power! While this is true, we often find it difficult to keep up with the amount of information and knowledge we need in order to be successful.

Your customers also face this knowledge gap which provides a unique opportunity to make knowledge transfer a competitive advantage for companies savvy enough capitalize on the opportunity. By freely sharing knowledge with your customers, you are enabling them to make better decisions and enhance their business capabilities. You are positioning your company as their trusted business advisor and solidifying the relationship against competitors. Adding real value also allows you to build a premium-pricing model that will contribute significantly more to your bottom line.

To actually transfer knowledge, managers must make learning a top priority, leading the way by becoming life long learners themselves. Compare your budget line items. What percentage of your budget is allocated for education? Is it as high as advertising, or marketing, or even client entertainment? Here comes the heretical statement: **Your education budget should be one of your largest investments!**

Notice that I said <u>investments</u>, not "costs." Costs don't return value to the organization; investments do, and so does education in a <u>big</u> way. Anyone who interfaces with the customer must be given every opportunity to attend training, seminars, and conferences. And not just education in your industry, or education related to one's role within the company (i.e., sales training for sales staff).

How can your staff transfer valuable knowledge to their customers if they don't know and understand their customer's industry? For instance, if your product or service is sold to the banking industry, your Account Managers should be attending the American Banking Association and Bank Administration Institute conferences and local events. These are opportunities for your Account Managers to learn about the banking industry, make networking contacts, and meet potential customers.

Account Managers should also understand how to manage and grow a business if they are to build credibility with their customer's senior management. How many business and industry journals come to your office? I'm just guessing, but if you do subscribe to the appropriate journals, I'm willing to bet there's just one copy for the whole office. It's time to get everyone his or her own subscription or, where possible, get an online subscription that everyone can access.

Act Now!

Start building deeper and more profitable customer relationships by taking these initial steps to building Strategic Account Managers who can become trusted advisors to your customers:

- Increase your education budget
- Subscribe to the appropriate periodicals and journals – get a subscription for each employee with customer face time
- Identify your key customer industries, research the top conferences and seminars in those industries, and assign attendance to your Account Managers
- Create opportunities to share information among your staff and in staff meetings
- Deliver Strategic Account Management training for all your sales reps (be sure it's customized to your needs and not off-the-shelf)
- Identify your best "trusted advisor" candidates and assign them your highest potential growth customers
- Develop a strategic account plan for each of your high-growth customers
- As management, demonstrate the behaviors you want in your staff – walk the talk!

Through strategic account management and knowledge sharing, you will begin to build the right relationships with your customers. You will realize the benefits of increased profitability, longer-term relationships, and pro-tection against competitors. What's more, you will gain knowledge that will help you improve not only your business, but that of your customers.

– Problem Resolution –

ACTION DRIVER ▶ *I Shouldn't Have To Beg!*
The French Revolution is Over

The attitude underlying Marie Antoinette's cry, "Let them eat cake!" spawned a revolution, a 1500-page book by Victor Hugo, and the enduring musical *Les Misérables*. This haughty display of indifference to those who begged for food brought down a monarchy.

Your customers should not have to beg for service. And they shouldn't have to ask for a supervisor – or God forbid, the supervisor's boss – to get a problem resolved. Hey big cable company monopoly – are you listening?! You're not?! Well, neither are many other big companies.

Delivering **superior service**, considered a goal by companies everywhere, starts after you've successfully delivered the basic service; it's giving the customer a fast and equitable resolution to his problem. If customers must beg for fairness by talking to layers of people before they get a satisfactory answer, you will never get to *superior*. You're stuck at *lousy*. So, what do you do?

- **Hire the right people for customer service.** Your CSRs need to speak with enthusiasm, act like they give a damn, and need to remember what it's like to be a customer. Personality test your CSR candidates to be sure they posses the appropriate personality and temperament before you risk your most important asset – your customers.

- **Hit them when they say, "It's not our policy."** Okay, so maybe you can't lay a hand on your CSRs, but how about a taser? I'm serious – this one little phrase will send a customer through the ceiling! It may in fact be your policy to do or not do something but, gee, maybe the policy is wrong! Or maybe, just maybe, in this instance ignoring the policy is best for business. Policies should be guidelines, not hammers for beating up customers.

- **Give your front line service staff <u>real</u> authority** to resolve 99% of the problems they receive. CSRs hate it when a customer says, "I want to speak to a supervisor." And why do customers jump to that request?! Because experience has taught them that the person who answers the phone can't or won't resolve their issue.

- **Train your CSR's in the basics of "service speak."** I am astounded daily by how many CSRs forget to use phrases like, "I'm sorry you've had this problem," or "I can understand how you must feel," or – the one <u>I</u> want to hear – "I promise that together we will resolve your problem. I really want to help."

I had an incident with the cable company that took me three phone calls, 72 minutes, and three layers of supervisors before an illegitimate charge was removed from my bill. No, the technician didn't fix the storm damage on Nov 6th – the repair guy came on Nov 8th. NO, he didn't come inside and install a splitter. Despite my corrections, all I heard over and over was, "We'll have to investigate," which I heard as "We believe you are lying and what our guy says goes."

But the most frightening thing I heard was this: "If I take that off your bill, I will be fired. Do you want me to lose my job?" At that moment I could guess that the big cable company's <u>policy</u> was to never remove a charge if a customer's version of events differed from the technician's (*Note: I repeat that I <u>could guess</u> this was the case, as in <u>allegedly</u> – my CYA for the legal beagles who may read this*).

You may not be in the consumer business *per se*, but your customers are consumers at other companies and the level of service they receive from the "other guy" will color their assessment of your service. So, be on your best behavior. Prepare your CSRs to be the exception – prepare them to deliver really great service, not just merely answer the phone. And give your service staff the authority and the knowledge they need to solve 99% of your customer's service requests – the best way to avoid the customer's guillotine.

– Problem Resolution –

ACTION DRIVER ▶ *I Am Unworthy! I Am a Mere Speck of Dirt*

How do I know this? Well, because I'm a frequent flyer. If the airlines live by the Golden Rule, I can only surmise that they and their employees wish to be treated roughly, without respect, and, in many instances, with outright derision and contempt. Boy, would I like to make their wishes come true!

I don't need to go into the litany of customer service failings of the airline industry. I would bet my entire fortune (small as it may be!) that you have your own horror stories to share. But as I travel, I am constantly reminded of 1) why I fly Jet Blue if at all possible, and 2) why customer complaint handling is <u>critical</u> to the health of our companies.

Just in case the CEOs of the other airlines are reading this... companies who care about their customers and their bottom line operate on several simple but profound customer service truths. Hey Mr. CEO: listen up! I'm going to share some wisdom:

> *The names of the offending airlines and their CEOs have been deleted to protect the innocent – ME! Both my lawyer and my bank account scream – no lawsuits!*

Brick Wall Breakthrough

When your company or an employee makes a mistake, there are three kinds of justice your customers **expect** and **deserve:**

1. An easy, convenient process to file a claim or ask for a resolution.

2. A sincere level of concern.

3. Fair compensation when appropriate.

Attention all airline executives: if you fail in any one of these areas, you risk a future customer. It is the combined experience in all of these arenas that determines how customers judge your performance. Studies have demonstrated that if a customer has to negotiate with you around compensation, she will ask for more than she would have if she hadn't had to negotiate. What's more, she will be more dissatisfied in the end, regardless of the level of compensation.

The lesson? **Offer the resolution or compensation quickly; do not make the customer work for it.**

A word to the wise... No, wait! The wise don't need a word – they get it!... Okay so a word to the stupid – yes Mr. Airline CEO, that's you: create performance standards for resolving complaints and **include standards for compensation.** Will the compensation be:

*   A refund for use later with your company?
*   A replacement?
*   Outright cash?

Next, set standards for the dollar amount for each above situation and define any discount that may be given as future compensation for today's screw-up. Want to minimize the size of any compensation? Don't make the customer ask for a supervisor or manager, get the manager to them immediately.

So, should the airlines have learned this Action Driver? Unhappy customers tell their tales of woe to lots and lots of people. Should this scare you enough to care? Yes! So take action and respect the customer, define an easy resolution process, accept responsibility, and fairly compensate customers when you screw up.

Raise your hands now: how many of you readers really believe Mr. Airline CEO gives a damn about us, their customers? Ah, yes there's always at least one optimist in every group! Well, I'm confident that you do care about your customers. And I'm just as confident you'll take action to insure **your employees live by the Golden Rule!**

Almost every religion and philosophy espouses some form of the Golden Rule. Why? Because when practiced, it solves everything. Here are a few versions:

Baha'i Faith *Lay not on any soul a load that you would not wish to be laid upon you, and desire not for anyone the things you would not desire for yourself.*

Buddhism *Treat not others in ways that you yourself would find hurtful.*

Christianity *So in everything, do to others as you would have them do to you, for this sums up the Law and the Prophets.*

Confucianism *One word which sums up the basis of all good conduct... loving-kindness. Do not do to others what you do not want done to yourself.*

Hinduism *This is the sum of duty: do naught unto others which would cause you pain if done to you.*

– Problem Resolution –

 *The Cowardly Lion*

"I'm afraid there's no denyin' / I'm just a dandy-lion / A fate I don't deserve. / I'm sure I could show my prowess / Be a lion, not a mouse / If I only had the nerve."*

You guessed it: the above words were sung by the Cowardly Lion in the *Wizard of Oz*. Despite his heritage as king of the jungle, this lion lacked courage. How much courage does your staff possess when it comes to coping with unhappy customers or clients? Do your employees own a mistake, face up to it, and fix it for the customer? Do they learn from it? They'd better!

In working with a salesperson for a large non-profit, I asked how a recent client meeting had gone. The salesperson replied: "It went great. The problem we had last month never came up. I feel like I dodged a bullet." After taking a deep, deep breath, I explained to the sales person that it was his responsibility to bring up the issue, discuss it, confirm that the client was satisfied with the resolution, and promise it would never happen again. But such action takes courage! If your employees lack this requisite courage, how do you help them build it?

Brick Wall Breakthrough

The Keys to Building a Courageous Staff

- Give your staff the ability and the <u>authority</u> to solve customer problems. If your employees always have to go to a superior, they will be less likely to accept responsibility for the resolution, <u>any</u> resolution.
- Encourage risk-taking by creating a safe landing, and coach your employees through the process.
- Give your staff opportunities to demonstrate courage when the stakes aren't as high, and praise them for being courageous.
- Reward honesty and personal responsibility.
- Create company policies and procedures that are built upon honesty.
- Most importantly, **lead by example**.

Your customers and/or clients expect and deserve to be treated with respect, honesty, and integrity. Admitting mistakes – especially <u>before</u> the customer raises the problem – and then quickly resolving them is the foundation for good customer service.

Years ago, while working as VP of Sales for a tech firm for a client who was one of the largest financial investment firms in the country, I learned a valuable service lesson. One of our staff members was arrogant and condescending to the students in a technology class. His behavior was rude and inexcusable. When the client called me to express her displeasure, I immediately

"It takes more courage to reveal insecurities than to hide them, more strength to relate to people than to dominate them, and more manhood to abide by thought-out principles rather then blind reflex."
- Alex Karras, American Football Player and Actor

apologized, assured her the instructor would be replaced the next day, and asked for the contact information for each student so that I could personally apologize. It was a humiliating and embarrassing experience, and the instructor was subsequently fired. But months later the client told me that she was impressed with the speed of our response, and most importantly, she was impressed that I didn't "pull the dodge" (her words) of saying I needed to speak with the instructor first before providing a resolution.

In my mind, it didn't matter what the instructor may or may not have said in his defense – our client was unhappy and <u>that</u> issue needed to be resolved immediately. The offending instructor later admitted his behavior, hence his termination, but even if he had been less at fault (for whatever reason), the original fact remained: the client was not happy.

It takes courage to admit your mistakes, take responsibility, and fix a problem, even if <u>you</u> didn't commit the mistake. Customers/clients expect you to demonstrate that courage and repair the relationship as quickly as possible. Your role as a leader is to build that courage into your team so that whenever and wherever a mistake occurs, the resolution is quick and straightforward. Imbue your team with the courage Dorothy displayed as she faced frightening odds of ever getting home.

– Deep Dives –

Customer Service

To learn more about the concepts discussed in the Customer Service Chapter of *Brick Wall Breakthrough*, consult these texts:

America's Service Meltdown, Restoring Service Excellence in the Age of the Customer, Raul Pupa (2002, Praeger).

Complaint Management Excellence, Creating Customers Loyalty Through Service Recovery, Sarah Cook (2012, Kogan Page).

Customer-Centered Growth: Five Strategies for Building Competitive Advantage, Richard Whiteley, Diane Hessan (1996, Addison Wesley).

Customer Intimacy: Pick Your Partners, Shape Your Culture, Win Together, Fred Wiersema (1998, Knowledge Exchange).

Delivering Knock Your Socks Off Service (Fifth Edition), Performance Research Associates (2011, AMACOM).

Exceptional Customer Service: Exceed Customer Expectation to Build Loyalty & Boost Profits, Lisa Ford, David McNair, Bill Perry (2009, Adams Media).

Brick Wall Breakthrough

Exceptional Service, Exceptional Profit: The Secrets of Building a Five Star Customer Service Organization, Leonard Inghilleri, Micah Solomon (2010, AMACOM).

High Tech, High Touch Customer Service, Micah Solomon (2012, AMACOM).

Managing Know Your Socks Off Service (Third Edition), Chip R. Bell, Ron Zemke (2011, AMACOM).

Powerful Phrases for Effective Customer Service: Over 700 Ready-to-Use Phrases and Scripts that Really Get Results, Renée Evenson (2012, AMACOM).

Service Excellence!, Price Pritchett (2007, Pritchett Publishing).

Service Recovery: Fixing Broken Customers (Management Master Series, 18), Ron Zemke (1996, Productivity Press).

Uncommon Service: How to Win by Putting Customers at the Core of Your Business, Frances Frei, Anne Morriss (2012, Harvard Business Review Press).

Unleashing Excellence: The Complete Guide to Ultimate Customer Service, Dennis Snow, Teri Yanovitch (2009, Wiley).

TALENT MANAGEMENT

– Recruiting –

 *Spinning the Roulette Wheel*

Finding the right person for the right job at the right time is as good as finding gold! But many companies are basically spinning the roulette wheel when they begin to search for sales talent. The results your sales team delivers on a day-to-day basis determine if there will in fact be another business day – dramatic, but absolutely true. Why then is such minimal effort expended on assessing sales candidates? Do you really think your gut is that good?

One of my earliest clients experienced the loss of a valuable leader to another organization. The culture within this organization was so unique that outside hires had not always been successful. So my client, a very forwarding-thinking president, made a daring decision to restructure her staff into "self-directed teams" to see whether leaders would "bubble to the top." While this experiment succeeded within this organization due to its culture of continuous learning, it is not a strategy I would recommend for most companies, especially in the sales arena.

The solution to finding your ideal sales candidate should be a **proactive strategy** that identifies existing talent and creates individual development plans to groom employees for future roles. Talent, skill, and aptitude assessments are increasingly more sophisticated and have become critical tools for management to use to uncover future leaders.

Brick Wall Breakthrough

Sales teams are effectively using such assessments to fill in skills gaps with new hires or to train current reps who can assume higher level sales responsibilities. Companies in transition from service to sales cultures, or from transaction selling to consultative selling, are increasingly turning to assessment tools to identify in-house talent before jumping to outside recruitment.

You can very effectively use assessments to:

- Develop a "sales competency model" based on the results from your top producers
- Build a team with the right mix of skills
- Plan for succession to crucial positions
- Target training with real precision

Great interviewing can also weed out the wrong candidates. Create an "interview guide" consisting of behavior-based questions to uncover the skills that match the sales process. Here's a sample of behavioral questions for each step in the sales process and the accompanying skills:

Sales Process Step	Competencies		Questions
Lead Generation	Detail-oriented Independent Inquisitive Technically Savvy	Thorough Organized Planner Persistent	• Can you give me an example of how you penetrated a new market or market segent? • How do you build leads? • Can you give me an example of an instance where you explored a new field or technology?
Qualifying	Approachability Self-confident Business Acumen Questioning Skills Interpersonal Skills Excellent Communicator	Flexible Proactive Competitive Self-motivated Great Listener	• What questions do you have about our business? • What three things would you want to know about a prospect before setting up an appointment?
Needs Assessment/ Discovery	Questioning Skills Business Acumen Industry Knowledge Product Knowledge Excellent Communicator Presentation Skills Listening Skills Responsiveness	Persistence Competitive	• How would you learn about a prospect's industry? • In your current industry, how would you determine a customer's need for your product/service? • Can you give me an example of where your questioning uncovered a need the client didn't see?
Solution Development	Detail-oriented Product Knowledge Writing Skills Time Management Listening Skills System Savvy Customer Industry Knowledge	Creative Organized	• Describe a situation in which your technical knowledge closed the sale. • What areas would you want to improve upon in order to be more successful? • Can you give an example of a particularly creative solution or proposal you developed for a customer?
Close	Creative Customer-focused Competitive Strong Negotiator Persuasiveness Persistence Results-oriented Proactive		• Can you give an example of a difficult-to-close prospect and how you succeeded? • When closing a sale, what points would you emphasize to the customer? • Can you give me an example of when your prices were higher than your competition but you still won the business? How did you do so?

Good interviewing skills and gut reactions are not good enough to build highly-effective teams, inside or outside of sales. Whether your challenge is replacing an employee, restructuring a department, or attracting new talent, well-researched, well-designed, and well-validated talent assessments are valuable tools in the fight against a shrinking workforce. Stop spinning the roulette wheel when hiring – the odds are no better in hiring real talent than in winning at the casino.

– Recruiting –

 *"We're All Bozos on This Bus!"*

The above title is taken from the Firesign Theater comedy album of the same name. It's another way of saying that success is achieved when you have the "right people on the bus." Why does this fundamental business truth elude so many managers – at all levels?

Every day, companies turn to outside consulting firms to solve a problem their inside experts are unable to resolve or that recurs despite focused attention. In too many instances, the root cause is traced to a "people problem," while the original request to the consulting firm was to improve revenue generation, fix a broken process that no one followed, repair customer satisfaction, or change company culture.

To achieve such goals, companies are willing to jettison products, markets, and business units. Companies might even acquire new products or new organizations. But when the solution is to discard non-performing staff and acquire the "right" staff, managers break into cold sweats and start their lists of excuses for not taking action.

Suck it up ladies and gentleman. To achieve real change, you may have to make personnel changes. As Nike says, "Just do it!" (legally and ethically, of course!). These *people problems* are two-fold: one is the nonperform-ing employees, the other is the managers who refuse to show some backbone and do what they are paid to do.

Get the right people on the bus! Before you call a consultant, take an immune system booster pill and get ready to fire your bozos and hire superstars. Here are the ten things you should do:

1. Justify your move on paper before you go to HR. Typically, HR departments are not risk takers.

2. Don't let inexperienced, timid, or traumatized HR professionals create unnecessary road blocks. Following the law and being humane do not translate into inaction.

3. Focus your search on finding the right person, not merely the right skills. Find the person whose attitude, ethics, approach, and philosophy match your mission and values. **The intangibles are what make the person right**. It is far more difficult, if not impos-sible, to get someone to change their beliefs. Skills, on the other hand, can be taught and nurtured, given the right foundation.

4. Build an interview strategy that is based on "behavioral ques-tioning" and includes interviews with colleagues and peers. Most people are pretty good at interviewing and can impress us on one, or even two, interviews. But faking it through a series of interviews is tough. Peer input is critical to maintaining ef-fective teams. Collaborative decision-making also shares the responsibility.

5. Use one of the many personality and/or competency tests that will give you a deeper picture than your impressions. Personality tests and competency tests are not the same thing: one tests for the right attitude, ethics, etc., the other for job-related skills and ability to be trained.

6. Plan for success. Create a mentoring/coaching plan for the new employee that transfers knowledge and skills, but also monitors his behavior, attitude, and drive.

7. Define your exit strategy. Cop shows have taught me to prepare for the worst. How long will you give the new person to prove their personality is a match? That their skills are strong enough? Hint: six months is too long! Start with clear, measurable, realistic goals and then hold the new employee accountable. Fix hiring mistakes quickly – not doing so is too high a loss in revenue, customer satisfaction, and morale.

8. Absolutely, positively document the new employee's weaknesses in reviews, letters, and verbal communication. Don't let the "well, he's new" syndrome prevent you from documenting the good, the bad, and the ugly. HR will demand it later.

9. Start searching for the right replacement before you fire! You should always be selling your company as a great place to work and interviewing good candidates regardless of the number of official job openings.

10. Reward your performers – keep them happy and clone them!

Brick Wall Breakthrough

The next time you have a business problem, start the evaluation by asking how people positively or negatively affect the issue. Would getting the right people on the bus solve the problem? If the answer is "yes," then ask why you haven't replaced certain people before? What do you need to do as a company to spur your managers into action? Having bozos on the bus is funny at Firesign Theater, but it's hardly humorous for a company that wants to thrive.

– Coaching –

 *It's the* Rocky Horror Picture Show

When you look around at your staff, does it scare you? Do they look more like Dr. Frank-N-Furter than Mark Zuckerberg? Do you see serious room for performance improvement? Do you wonder why your talented management team is not doing a better job of developing its staff?

News flash! One cause of less-than-stellar staff development can be found in annual performance reviews: once-a-year reviews result in once-a-year feedback on performance and once-a-year promises from the employee that he'll change. Very little behavior change results from a once-a-year feedback approach.

You say, "But my managers give feedback all year long! Their employees know exactly where they stand and what is expected of them." I'll bet they do. I'd put money down that your managers are providing "directional feedback" versus more effective *developmental feedback* practiced as by managers who <u>coach</u> their teams. Your managers are telling their teams exactly what to do, how to do it, and what happens if they don't.

 Try **coaching for performance** instead of *managing* for performance. There is a huge difference between the two methods:

Brick Wall Breakthrough

A coaching conversation is structured to get the employee to see his challenges versus being told what those challenges are. Coaching conversations help the employee find his own solution to removing road blocks to behavior change versus being told what not to do. In a true coaching conversation, the manager doesn't prescribe, she asks questions to lead the employee to enlightenment. Real behavior change occurs when the employee, with support from the coach, owns his weakness and finds his own solution to changing his behavior.

Ownership is critical. No one changes if he doesn't believe he owns his behavior. When you manage an employee, you take away his ownership and thus remove the probability of lasting change.

Effective coaching conversations have several steps:

1. Non-judgmental opening statement

2. Discovery

3. Developmental feedback

4. Action plan

5. Removal of obstacles to the new behavior

6. Follow-up plan

Opening Statement. Your opening statement should state the purpose of the coaching conversation in a non-threatening way. Say, "I would like to discuss your last customer conversation in particular around our liability product," instead of the more threatening and emotional statement, "I'm very upset about that customer conversation; you didn't know anything about our liability products." Your opening sets the tone for the entire conversation.

Discovery. The discovery step is where managing and coaching diverge. In coaching, you ask questions to uncover the facts about the current behavior, beliefs, and habits of the employee. **It is all about asking, not telling**. Ask at least three questions, such as: How do you think that went? What's going on? What happened with x event? What did you do well? What do you believe is getting in the way of your knowledge of our liability products?

Developmental Feedback. Once you've asked the questions, **let the employee talk – uninterrupted**! When he is done, give him <u>developmental</u> feedback, not directional feedback. Directional feedback is focused on the past, usually contains a judgment, and begins with "you." On the other hand, *developmental feedback* is focused on <u>future</u> behavior, reflects things the coachee may not realize about his words or behavior, and begins with "we." Developmental feedback is observational, not judgmental. Give feedback on what the coachee has just told you about the issue. Offer a response like: "I know you're trying and you have attended product training, but something is getting in the way of expressing your knowledge. What do you think that might be? I hear your explanation for this, but I wonder what part in this is yours?"

Action Plan. Together, develop a plan for how the employee will change his behavior. How will he demonstrate the new behavior and in what time frame? Discuss what he will do differently and ensure that <u>he</u> develops the plan. Remember, coaching is asking not telling, i.e., asking "What can you do to show the client you know our products?" versus "At the next client meeting I want you to at least list the benefits of our liability product."

Remove the Obstacles and Follow Up. If the employee protests and says he can't make the change because of [fill in the blank], work together to remove that obstacle. Again, ask him what he thinks needs to happen to make it possible to adjust his behavior. After that discussion, schedule the follow-up coaching session - <u>never</u> leave it open ended! What doesn't get scheduled, doesn't get done. Consistency and follow-up are critical to seeing the change, supporting the change, and sustaining the change.

Managing is always necessary. It will always be necessary to tell employees what to do and how well you expect them to do it. But telling someone to change her behavior rarely elicits the results you want. Coaching your team to change will generate results faster and it will generate lasting, sustainable change.

– Coaching –

ACTION DRIVER ▶ *Here I Am at Camp Grenada*

You can hear them from across the lake: the voices of over 100 boys, ages 13 to 16, who are attending camp for six weeks. No, it's not really Camp Grenada, that mythical sleep-away in the like-titled comedy song, but it's as close as you can get. Camp Wildwood on Woods Pond in Bridgton, Maine, has been teaching kids to swim, ski, and canoe for almost 100 years. As I sit on my dock and watch the kids try to tip a canoe, then right it again, I realize that we executives and managers could learn a lot from Camp Wildwood's approach to teaching.

Camp Wildwood practices a very simple methodology:

1. Give clear instructions

2. Give plenty of opportunity to try a new skill

3. Let kids fail, without dire consequences (like drowning)

4. Coach and encourage, from first attempt through mastery

Each Wildwood two-kid canoe team has a guide in a boat next to them as they tip the canoe and attempt to right it. RIGHT NEXT TO THEM.

Brick Wall Breakthrough

Not back on the beach in a counselors' meeting, or off doing other camp business: within an arm's reach.

With the exception of a new employee, managers often assign a new project, open a new market, introduce a new product, or just plain tell employees how to improve without getting in the boat with them or next to them. What's worse, we expect them to do the job perfectly the first time, with little to no coaching.

Active coaching is relegated to the "when I can" calendar, but the consequences of failing to actively coach are detrimental to your bottom line. It is especially important to coach your front line staff – the sales and customer service warriors. When they make mistakes, you lose customers. When was the last time you spent a day with your sales team making calls or presentations? How long has it been since you listened in on those customer service interactions? Not just listening to taped conversations, but sitting beside the CSR – live! Effective coaching is "in the moment." It's before you send the campers out in the lake; it's <u>during</u> the demonstration of what to do. It's when the canoe has tipped over, the campers are struggling, getting tired, and ready to give up. Following the simple coaching rules of Camp Wildwood at your organization will develop truly committed professionals who'll deliver at peak performance.

– Training –

ACTION DRIVER ▶ *I Sell – You Hire – and Never the Twain Shall Meet*

Who develops and delivers sales training for your company? Are you large enough to have an HR department, but not large enough to have an experienced sales professional in a training role? In many companies, developing and delivering sales training falls to someone in the HR department.

> *Disclaimer: I firmly believe that selling should be taught by someone who has... well, actually sold something, but let's accept that this doesn't always happen.*

So, without an experienced sales trainer, your HR person may feel challenged by the prospect of designing sales training. After all, sales people are often viewed as an alien species, a necessary evil in the eyes of non-sales people. In addition, many in sales management agree that "if you haven't been in the trenches selling," you can't possibly design an effective sales training program.

While there is some truth to both of these opinions, non-selling HR professionals can design effective sales training. So, get together with your HR professional and study this guide to make it happen.

Brick Wall Breakthrough

For the HR professional, designing sales training requires more than asking standard questions about weaknesses in the sales team. You will need to assume the role of "internal consultant" and work with your sales management team to develop a relevant and sustaining sales training program. By following the four-step program outlined here, you can establish your credibility with sales management and demonstrate that design is a collaborative effort.

Four Steps to Designing Effective Sales Training Programs

| Defining the Sales Role | Mapping the Sales Process | Identifing Sales skills | Assessing Skills |

Ultimately, any training program should introduce the skills required to be successful in a particular job function. The complexity of the sales function, however, can make the skills definition more difficult. Accurately and clearly defining which sales skills should be the focus of the training takes careful evaluation using the four steps presented above.

Step #1: Defining the Sales Role. Not all sales roles have the same focus or goal and understanding your sales team's roles is vital to developing relevant and lasting training. There are three aspects of a sales role that must be identified:

a) <u>The sales goal for that role.</u> Is the goal retention, expansion, acquisition, or partner development? Sales goals are not as simple as "increase revenue" or "meet this dollar or margin goal." While the ultimate goal is financial, the sales person's actions, and thus the skills he needs, are dependent upon his focus; examples include retaining customers, expanding the existing customer

relationship, acquiring new customers, and building relationships with partners that will sell for you.

b) <u>The direction of the sales role.</u> Is the team an outbound-selling
team or is it an inbound team? Outbound sales teams are considered "street specialists," even if their territory is worldwide.
They sell by physically meeting with customers. Alternatively,
the role of an inbound team can be defined as either:

- Prospecting and lead generation only, referring the leads to the
outbound sales team to close.
- Calling a specific targeted list with reps closing sales themselves.
- Taking inbound calls from customers and closing the sale.

The skills for outbound and inbound sales will be similar, but their
focus is likely to be on a limited subset of more general sales skills.

c) <u>Is the focus of the selling direct or indirect.</u> Is the sales team selling directly to the end customer, or is the sales team selling to
channel partners who conduct the direct sale and manage the
end customer relationship?

Understanding the specific sales roles within your organization will
impact the next step in the design process: defining and mapping your
organization's sales process.

Step #2: Mapping the Sales Process. Every sales person follows a sales
process. It may be well-defined and well-understood, or it may be driven
by trial and error or instinct. For better or worse, however, a process
does exist.

Brick Wall Breakthrough

The best sales departments have a defined and documented sales process based on best practices gleaned from their own history or industry standards. That defined process should then be tracked and driven by Customer Relationship Management or Sales Enablement Software. As the curriculum designer, you will need to understand and map that sales process. If your sales department has never taken the time to define and document its sales process, then your role as an internal consultant has just become more valuable. You can drive this vital exercise and play a pivotal role in the process. Understanding the sales process gives the sales team and its management the knowledge necessary to duplicate success and prevent failure.

Basic Sales Process

| Prospect/ Lead Generation | Qualifying/ Approach | Discovery/ Needs Assessment | Solution Development | Close | Manage |

Mapping will itemize the actions required of sales people for each step in the process and thus allow you to identify the skills required for its successful execution.

NOTE: When you define the sales process, take advantage of the opportunity to fine-tune and improve upon your current plan. The first round should be an "as is" map of the process, which transforms into the "future" map after sales management has evaluated and adjusted the process for higher success.

Step #3: Identifying the Skills. Using the map of your company's specific sales process and the actions required under each step, you can now begin to **identify the specific skills** required to execute each action under each step. At this point in the training design, the sales process should be more about <u>how</u> to move through the process rather than the what of the process, so thoroughly list the <u>real</u> actions sales people should take to be successful. Here is an example of the skills matrix:

Sales Process and Corresponding Competencies

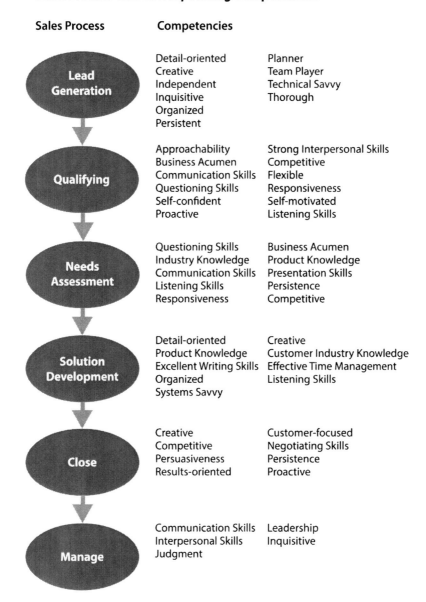

Sales Process	Competencies	
Lead Generation	Detail-oriented Creative Independent Inquisitive Organized Persistent	Planner Team Player Technical Savvy Thorough
Qualifying	Approachability Business Acumen Communication Skills Questioning Skills Self-confident Proactive	Strong Interpersonal Skills Competitive Flexible Responsiveness Self-motivated Listening Skills
Needs Assessment	Questioning Skills Industry Knowledge Communication Skills Listening Skills Responsiveness	Business Acumen Product Knowledge Presentation Skills Persistence Competitive
Solution Development	Detail-oriented Product Knowledge Excellent Writing Skills Organized Systems Savvy	Creative Customer Industry Knowledge Effective Time Management Listening Skills
Close	Creative Competitive Persuasiveness Results-oriented	Customer-focused Negotiating Skills Persistence Proactive
Manage	Communication Skills Interpersonal Skills Judgment	Leadership Inquisitive

Step #4: Assessing the Skills. Identifying the skills required for your company to be successful in sales is not the end of the training design. Effective training is customized and targeted, and thus must focus on the right skills, not all the skills.

Each sales person should be assessed for her competency in each skill. Aggregating the results will tell you where the members of the team have common strengths and weaknesses. In consultation with sales management, you can determine which skills are most influential in ensuring success. This information, coupled with the common weaknesses, will determine which skills should be the focus of your training design.

Where individuals have unique weaknesses, coaching and individual training are appropriate. Building training upon the lowest common denominator frustrates your good salespeople and alienates your best ones.

Conclusion

Sales training design is a process that anyone can master and deploy. Using the process described here ensures that non-sales people are successful at designing the content and focus of effective training. Your biggest challenge now becomes "Who should facilitate the training?"

The best sales training is delivered by sales pros who have been there/done that – successfully. But also understand that their way is not the only way. Sales training should introduce skills, concepts, and exercises to practice the skills and real life scenarios relevant to your industry and customers. Facilitators or trainers should introduce real life tips and tricks, but must not demand conformity to their selling style or approach.

There is room for individuality in executing the steps of the sales process. Facilitators who see training as a pulpit from which to preach their truth are doomed to deliver irrelevant training. Using the four steps above, in conjunction with proper preparation, will empower you to find the right facilitator for the job and ensure that the introduced skills are effectively implemented.

– Training –

ACTION DRIVER ▶ *One Size Doesn't Fit All!*
Selecting a Training Partner

I'm not sure where the phrase "one size fits all" originated, but I bet it was a marketing creation designed to convince a buyer that one standard, mass-produced item would meet both her need <u>and</u> those of all humanity. Great concept if you're the seller, but destined to produce an unhappy, dissatisfied buyer.

Buying packaged, off-the-shelf sales training can be as disastrous as buying a "one size fits all" tuxedo for the boss's Christmas party. It looks great at first glance, but closer inspection of the oversized sleeves and too short pants makes a bad impression – not the result you were hoping for.

Selecting the right sales training for your company is the result of a careful examination of your goals and an honest appraisal of your staff's current strengths and weaknesses. Sales training delivered in isolation from your company's goals and strategies will fail to deliver the desired results. You want a skilled sales force armed with the appropriate tools and knowledge to increase revenue and improve margins! And remember, training is only <u>one</u> building block of a great sales culture that will produce and support highly-effective sales professionals.

Brick Wall Breakthrough

Selecting the Right Sales Training Requires Alignment

For any sales training program to be effective and deliver lasting results it must be aligned with your company's:

- Financial Goals
- Growth Strategy
- Sales Strategy
- Industry
- Culture

Aligned With Financial Goals

This one is simple. You say, "We want our sales force to drive revenue and deliver yearly increases." Driving revenue is just one financial goal, but it isn't always the <u>appropriate</u> goal.

Too many companies go out of business by solely focusing on driving revenue. If increasing your market share is the primary goal, sales training that focuses on selling against the competition and closing any deal would meet your need.

But delivering the "right" business drives higher margins, and this goal requires a sales force with skills and knowledge above just being closers. Building the business around higher margins requires higher-level sales relationships and the ability to sell based on customer needs.

Aligned with Growth Strategy

What happens to companies that don't grow? They stagnate and eventually wither. This truism means that every company desires growth. But how you choose to grow affects the content and the focus of your sales training program.

If your growth strategy is to focus on acquiring new accounts, your sales team must be expert at prospecting, backed by a marketing strategy that produces leads and gives reps a competitive advantage. If your growth strategy is to focus on an industry vertical, success will be determined by the industry knowledge and experience possessed by your sales team. When account penetration is your growth strategy, your sales professionals must be able to sell "value" through a consultative approach.

Aligned with Sales Strategy

Your growth strategy determines your sales strategy which, in turn, impacts the type of sales training you select. A *product-focused sales strategy* requires an in-depth knowledge of not only your products, but those of your competitors.

Product-focused selling is often the preferred approach for companies with limited product lines or for industries where there are no opportunities to up-sell or sell additional services. This approach means sales reps must "close and close now" – service and long-term relationships are not important. Telephone sales require this aggressive, close-at-all-costs culture.

Training for this team has a very different content and approach than for a team that must build relationships. Sales strategies designed to foster long-term relationships and account penetration can only be successful when training teaches how to become a *trusted advisor*, i.e., how to become the consultant customers depend upon to meet their needs and further their goals.

Brick Wall Breakthrough

Aligned with Your Industry

Sales is sales is sales! True or False? The politically correct answer is "true"; sales skills can be applied across any industry.

But the real answer is that <u>how</u> you apply these skills is unique to each industry. How and why your customers buy your services establishes how you should sell to them. Buyers of life insurance and financial services buy to protect themselves and their families. When purchasing education, particularly advanced education, buyers do so to advance careers, and perhaps egos. How you sell to your customers should be based on an understanding of buyer styles, buyer influences, and buyer decision factors. Your sales training provider should know and understand your industry.

Aligned with Your Organizational Culture

How would you describe your culture to an outsider:

- Fast-paced?
- Aggressive?
- Driven?
- Relaxed?
- Methodical?
- Risk-taking?
- Customer-focused?
- Change-adverse?

Sales training must factor into your organization's unique culture. You have two choices when considering how your sales training should respond to your culture: tailor the sales style to your current culture, or use sales training as a catalyst to change your existing culture. In either case, you should consciously evaluate this aspect – your "cultural goal" for sales training is critical to success during and after the training.

– Training –

 *Not So Fast!*

It's Friday afternoon. You've just left a long, contentious meeting in which lackluster revenue was the main topic. Your team suggested several actions, but you need to clear your head and think hard before acting. With a headache creeping up on you, you walk through your customer service area and hear, "Hey Man, that's not our fault. We don't control UPS. I can't help it if they delivered the product two days late. On your next order, I think you should do overnight shipping instead of two-day, that way your chances of getting the shipment on time are pretty good."

"Oh sh*t," you say to yourself. "Another problem." Then you think, "I need to fix this! We need to get these guys customer service training!" So you tell your VP of Sales to get a trainer in fast and improve the company's customer service. But wait! NOT SO FAST!

How will you evaluate and determine the content of that overdue training? And is training alone the answer?

Let's tackle the latter question first: no, training alone is not the answer. Customer service problems are <u>never</u> just about the people delivering the service. They're about your culture, policies, procedures, and processes, as well as how well you understand your customer's needs.

Brick Wall Breakthrough

The customer service Action Drivers in the previous section of this guide address these issues, so right now let's focus on what defines effective customer service training.

Effective customer service training content must include:

- **Decision-making skills.** You can't plan for every customer situation or issue. One of the worst things you can do is to ask a trainer to develop scripts for everyone to follow. Not only will your CSRs sound like robots, but your customer will receive very little of the empathy they need and deserve.

  Training should include a discussion surrounding the decisions your frontline staff has the authority to make and those in which they should seek approval. Training should teach CSRs the appropriate decision criteria so they will make the right decision for the customer and for the company. In other words, you want them to **think of, not just recite, a prescribed response**.

- **Understanding basic customer needs and expectations.** Decision-making must be based on a fundamental understanding of the basic customer needs and expectations. Too much customer service training is prescriptive and ignores conceptual insights such as customer needs, wants, and expectations, as well as how customers rate a service experience. Prescribed solutions or scripts don't provide a foundation upon which to make decisions that will keep a customer happy. Don't ignore the fundamentals. They may not feel as action-driven as detailed responses for each situation, but they are the key to managing the individuality of customers and the diverse situations your customer service team encounters.

- **Self-awareness.** Your CSRs should understand how they respond to stress, pressure, and requests from challenging customers. When faced with difficulty, do they flee or stand up? It's the old fight or flight syndrome.

  By understanding her natural inclination, the employee can learn not to become aggressive or run to a supervisor when pushed, and instead develop strength in difficult customer situations. Training your employees to understand their own behavior tendencies, and to compensate for such, will improve your company's overall customer satisfaction levels.

- **Behavior mirroring skills.** Self-awareness is the first step in understanding the behavior patterns within a customer conversation. The second step is to understand the communication style of your customer and adjust your style to match hers.

  A very simple example is knowing when to keep explanations short and when to give the customer extra reassurance. Human nature says we are more comfortable working with people like us. Learning how to uncover your customer's style, then matching it, builds trust and speeds toward the right solution.

- **Customization.** Generic customer service training does have positive effects but it will only last about 30 days, and then it's right back to old behavior. Generic customer service training places the burden upon the employees to translate the generic concepts to their real world – not a great idea if they are in training to improve subpar performance.

The best customer service training is based on your customers' specific needs and their assessment of your service. Your training partner should interview customers and assess the capabilities of the service team before developing content that is unique to your company, product, and customers.

Despite your Friday afternoon shock and desire to act, don't act too quickly as you evaluate training options. Lasting behavior change is your ultimate goal. Achieving that goal and sustaining the results are products of careful planning and honest reflection about the team, your company, and, most importantly, your customers.

– Termination –

ACTION DRIVER ▶ *Oh Yeah?*
What Are You Going To Do About It!

In varying ways, clients continually pose this question: "I can't get Felicia to file her reports on time. I've talked to her about it over and over. We've given her time management training and coaching and she still can't seem to get things done. How do I get her to do what I ask?"

The answer is either **"Fire 'em up!"** or **"Fire them out!"** You only have two choices. Regardless of which you take, you <u>must</u> hold the person accountable for her actions or, in Felicia's case, her non-action. Accountability is one of the hardest skills to master as a leader – but master it you must.

It's time for some soul searching. Why might you find it hard to hold people's feet to the fire? Is it fear? Fear of what? Which one of these fears is preventing you from building a culture of accountability:

- **Fear of not being liked**? Everyone wants to be liked; some see taking a stand or drawing a line in the sand as demanding or even dictatorial. But I ask, "As the boss, who else is going to demand excellence?!" There's a difference between "liking" someone and "respecting" someone. As a leader you need respect – skip the Facebook like!

- **Fear of conflict**? Because getting wounded is a possibility in conflict, some take the path of least resistance. They might keep telling Felicia over and over to do what needs to be done and hope that one day she will change her spots. Fight or flight! As the leader of your company, you actually control and reduce the level of conflict in your office by being decisive. Remember, non-performing employees negatively impact those around them! Failure to face the conflict these employees create leads to morale issues and reduces productivity throughout your company.

- **Fear of the consequences?** Establishing and enforcing consequences for non-performance is difficult, and perhaps the real fear is what might happen if you do: will the employee resign? Will I have to recruit, hire, and train again?

All the policies, procedures and processes in the world won't get recalcitrant, under-performing employees to do as you expect – and by the way, neither will just training! You need a plan for accountability. So, here are the steps you should take to insure accountability, yours and theirs:

- **Begin with consequences.** If your employees don't know or don't believe there will be serious consequences for their actions, the rest of these steps are meaningless at best. Clearly communicate the consequences: "Felicia, here at Socks R Us we believe that keeping our customers happy takes hard work from all our staff members. Failing to own your responsibilities and execute them effectively will jeopardize your employment."

- **Set clear, measurable expectations.** Don't be wishy-washy and generalize: "We need you to be proactive. We need you to respect your coworkers." Be very clear: "Felicia, at Socks R Us we believe that employees are happiest when they know exactly how to build customer loyalty. So let's be clear about what our customers, and what I, expect from you as our first female Sock Wrangler." Then state the specifics: "Felicia you show respect for coworkers by supporting them, not demeaning them with negative language. We require that you follow company policies and procedures such as our 15-minute break time policy."

- **Secure employees' buy-in.** Get Felicia to verbally agree to her role and responsibilities and to understanding the consequences of non-performance. Only time will tell if Felicia is really willing to own her performance, but at least you've laid the foundation.

- **Measure performance.** Consistent, formal performance evaluations are important for driving desired behavior, but they are critical to dealing with subpar performance.

- **Coach the person and give her actionable feedback.** Give your employee opportunities to own her work, to improve, or to "get" it. **But this does not take years!** If employees who've been with you for longer than 12 months are still not performing beyond "barely adequate," despite coaching, mentoring, performance conversations, and loads of positive feedback and reinforcement, then fire 'em out! Firing them up clearly isn't working.

- **Hold yourself accountable.** Strong leadership requires guts. Leadership ain't for sissies. Being a good leader means doing the dirty work. It means you may not always be liked. It means overcoming your fears and taking action and it may mean firing someone.

Brick Wall Breakthrough

Experience has demonstrated that there's always a good person out there looking for work. Don't let that fear-inducing voice in your head tell you that you'll never find anyone good to replace Felicia because he won't know the uniqueness of your industry, your quirky payroll system, etc. How good is Felicia anyway if she won't do what you ask? Any eager, smart, hard-working, success-oriented individual will trump Felicia any day. As long as your compensation is market-driven, your business is respected, and your product is desirable, you <u>will</u> find a better Sock Wrangler.

So let go of the fear. Stop losing money by allowing your non-performing employees to bully you into inaction. Take back your business!

– Termination –

 *C... Y... A...*

Economic drivers are certainly forcing businesses to reduce costs and layoffs are one way of saving money. Ideally, layoffs should target non-performers rather than cut staff across the board.

But, it is never easy to lay off people. The emotional aspects often over-shadow the needs of the business. And quite frankly, laying off sales people is particularly tricky. In working with a client who was preparing to lay off sales people, my advice was to conduct a "sales risk assess-ment" before pulling the trigger.

A *sales risk assessment* will uncover all of your areas of vulnerability should the terminated employee decide to "pay you back" for setting him free. There are specific actions you should take to protect your company, not just from legal challenges, but to protect your "sales intel-lectual property." Remember, terminating a sales person is vastly more complicated than terminating others in the company – sales people are the direct connection to your most important asset: your customers.

The first element of the risk assessment is to clearly define why this person is being let go and to review the facts to support your position, especially facts that are in writing. Then do a cost/benefit analysis to understand the upside and downside of the action you're about to take.

Brick Wall Breakthrough

This following **Termination Checklist** raises the critical issues you should consider when terminating any employee. It is by no means comprehensive and I would always advise a client to seek legal advice before termination to insure adherence to any applicable state and federal laws But working with the Checklist is the <u>minimum</u> you should do - it's all about covering your a**!

How to Use the Checklist

The checklist is divided into separate categories with actions under each area of responsibility. Senior management should use the checklist as a method of assigning responsibility for resolution of the issues raised. You may wish to have specific department managers execute their respective areas and report back to senior management who will record the action on the checklist to insure all action is captured in one document.

While this risk assessment is targeted for the termination of a sales person, you can edit it for any employee type.

Termination Checklist

Replacement Strategy (if this is not a layoff)?

Recruitment strategy in place before employee terminated?

Position competencies defined?

Job description updated?

Compensation plan reviewed and updated?

Territories reviewed and redefined as necessary?

Interviewing process and behavioral interview questions drafted?

Financial repercussions?

Plan for tracking, calculating, and paying outstanding commissions?

"Commissions due" report prepared for terminated employee?

A "collections" report generated and assigned for collections?

Report on expected lost business developed?

Appropriate memberships or subscriptions canceled?

Final expense report strategy developed?

Mobile device contracts canceled or transferred?

Company car, keys, and credit cards returned?

Severance payment plan developed and communicated to employee?

Continuing benefits plan developed and communicated to employee?

– The Other Kind of Change –

ACTION DRIVER ▶ *It's Coming! Scared Yet?*

There are very few things that scare us more than change. When the doctor says "exercise more," we respond with a list of reasons why we don't have the time. When it's time to install new or upgraded software, your end users are quick to scream about lost productivity while learning it. Change is necessary, but it's a monster at the door, instilling fear, panic, and resistance – just ask my colleagues how I responded to Windows 8!

Change is serious business; as leaders, you must prepare your company for the inevitable. Before beginning any change initiative, your company must first assess its readiness. Knowing how well the company will respond to the change gives learning leaders an advance understanding of the unique roadblocks before them and allows them to plan a strategy to keep moving forward.

A *readiness assessment* should uncover:

- Gaps between management's and employees' perceptions about the company's culture
- Gaps between the stated vision and values of the organization and how business is executed
- Gaps between the current culture and the desired elements of the new culture

- Degree of flexibility, adaptability, and innovation within the organization

Many organizational elements should be examined in a readiness assessment:

Key Performance Indicators (KPIs) must begin with a clear understanding of where the company is going and how you'll know when it's gotten there. KPIs must be established in three areas:

"It is not the strongest species that survive, nor the most intelligent, but the ones most responsive to change."
- Charles Darwin

1. **Performance:** which includes productivity, efficiency, and internal and external customer satisfaction

2. **Culture:** which refers to organizational behavior, values, and decisions

3. **Fiscal:** which relates to profitability, cost reduction, and market position

Each company's ultimate change goal will determine these KPIs and provide the tactical road map needed to take action and evaluate interim progress.

Risk Tolerance. Change involves risk. Up and down the organization, trust must be present if employees are going to take risks — not wild, poorly-conceived risks, but the calculated risks necessary to implement change.

Therefore, a company's willingness to allow risk-taking — and at times, failure — is one of the most important indicators of its change readiness.

How does the company view risk? How does it manage risk? What levels of risk are acceptable? Is an entrepreneurial spirit rewarded?

Decision-Making. All decisions, big and small, become the drivers of change. When change initiatives fail, it's often due to the fear of making a mistake, which leads to poor, and slow, decision-making.

Therefore, examining how decisions are made is vitally important. Company executives should ask: are decisions made quickly after fact finding and evaluation, or does it take longer for someone to make a decision and take action? Do the various management teams listen to a variety of opinions, or do they go to the "anointed few" for input? Is there a clear decision-making process?

Organizational Structure. Companies with very strong and delineated hierarchies were often built upon the belief that people need close supervision in order to get them to produce. Micromanagement is the norm. However, effective change initiatives require independent decision-making and behavior. Change that is forced on people is never fully adopted, and resistance becomes a huge challenge. If employees feel they can't make a move without approval, the organization will find change extremely difficult – if not impossible – to achieve.

Flexibility and Innovation. Flexibility and innovation are closely tied to risk. Leaders should ask themselves: "How often does my company attempt new things? Are new products introduced regularly? Are policies and procedures evaluated regularly to insure customer satisfaction? Is customer input solicited and is action taken based on those results? Do the employees implement new ideas on a consistent basis? Are employees allowed or encouraged to make decisions and solve problems within their own departments?"

Brick Wall Breakthrough

The most innovative companies have experienced failure. They assessed the risk and took the chance – in some instances because doing nothing is riskier. Apple, Facebook, and Google are just a few examples of companies that understood "nothing ventured nothing gained."

Change History. Past achievements can be indicators of future success. Has the company implemented some form of change within the last five years? Was it successful? What was learned from that experience? Was a change readiness assessment completed before the change initiative? What failures has the company experienced in the last five years and how can the company mitigate a failure mentality?

You can't change your past history, but the axiom that those who "fail to learn from history are doomed to repeat it" is absolutely true when attempting organizational change. Learn from your past mistakes and build a better outcome this time around.

Processes and Function. Major change often requires redesigning processes, functions, and roles. Are the managers in the affected area open to change? Are they supportive of the change? Is turf building and protection an issue? Do departments willingly collaborate and see themselves as interdependent? Are departments mired in paperwork that will work against change?

When a process change is the goal, it is wise to include those who manage or depend upon the process in the evaluation and solution. Don't forget your customers in process change. Process that may seem only internally-focused almost always have a way of touching the customer.

Communication. Communication before, during, and after change is critical to the success of a change initiative. Leaders must honestly assess both formal and informal communication structures within the organization. Is communication a two-way street with honest dialogue? Or is gossip rampant and destructive? Are trusted communicators maximized for the dissemination of information? Is communication direct or received only through managers? How frequently does senior management communicate with and listen to the rank and file?

Gaps in information give rise to fear and gossip that will doom any change initiative. Success depends upon everyone receiving all the information and at the same time. When one department hears about the change before another, you handcuff yourself by creating division when unison is the goal.

Competitive Awareness. Change in a vacuum is difficult. Do key people in the company stay informed about the industry? Do they track trends and see the impact on business? Are they knowledgeable about the competition and their position in the market?

The more employees know about the industry, the more they will understand the need for change and the benefits that change will deliver.

Rewards. A company's reward structure drives behavior. Are employees rewarded for new ideas, for taking risks, and for making independent decisions? Or are they "slapped" for taking action without multiple approvals?

The behavior you reward is the behavior you'll see — so make sure you reward the underlying actions that will support your change initiative.

– The Other Kind of Change –

ACTION DRIVER ▶ *Superman or Merely Human: What Kind of Change Leader Are You?*

Truly customer-driven organizations understand that listening to their customers means *change*. Change in people, processes, and systems. Change in the internal processes that make it easier for their customer to do business with <u>them</u> instead of competitors. Change that drives the creation of new products and services to better meet their customers' needs and desires. Change in metrics that define and drive performance. Real, tangible, and lasting changes must take place while organizations become better builders of profitable customer relationships.

How do you manage simultaneous change across the organization? How do you lead an organization when you feel like you're drowning in a sea of constant, rapid change? Is it possible to survive and thrive with change?

The answer to all these questions is "Yes!" Surviving change is difficult, so it will take some effort to manage and embrace that change.

Change is No Longer Linear

In the past, change was linear. You could deal with changes one at a time, as they arose. Employees and managers had at least some time to adjust and adapt to change.

Brick Wall Breakthrough

But in today's business environment, changes are occurring <u>across</u> the organization simultaneously. Sales is installing new CRM software while adjusting data and reporting for the new system. Billing is introducing a new process for speeding up the customer invoice process, in hopes of reducing your Days Sales Outstanding (DSO) timeline. Production just jumped on the Six Sigma bandwagon, letting loose the process improvement missionaries.

What happens when the volume and speed of change is this great? In face of things seemingly out of our control, the old "fight or flight' rule often takes over. Employees who feel overwhelmed often resist the change or, if fighting back is not part of their personality, may literally flee the change by leaving the company or department. As humans, we can adjust to only so much change while still accepting and adapting to it.

So, as a manager or leader of change, does this mean you should await calm before introducing more change, regardless of the need? No. I would <u>not</u> wait if I were you because there is no such thing as "the calm before the storm" anymore. Change is one big storm these days and we need to learn to lead our teams and companies through the continuous storm of change.

Becoming a Successful Change Leader

To become a successful leader of change, which will help both you and your organization weather the storm, consider these basic steps:

1. **Throw Away your Superman Costume.** Resist the temptation to do it all. You can't hold everyone's hand, you can't solve every problem, and you can't manage all the simultaneous changes. Identify those employees who have demonstrated that they

can survive and lead through change and assign them goals and responsibilities. This is a unique opportunity to build and strengthen future leaders. Your company's future depends on experienced leaders who know they can and will be successful despite constant change.

2. **Master the Change Process.** Successful change leaders know what to expect and can see trouble coming a mile away. You should study the change process and be prepared to guide your team through it. You need to understand the effects of change and address them, especially in regard to "fight or flight."

3. **Personally Embrace Change.** You must set the example by keeping a positive attitude and focusing on the change's objectives and results, not its problems. You need to be organized and proactive during the more stressful periods of change, and you must remain flexible. Resilience is an important virtue practiced by successful change leaders.

4. **Align the Change to the Organizational Strategy.** To avoid the feeling of "change for change's sake" among your employees, make sure they clearly understand the reasons for the change, that an ultimate good will come of out the seeming chaos. Leaders should focus on the organization's business imperatives and goals and not get lost in the "newest good idea." Change must always advance the business strategy and demonstrate results that directly and positively impact your customer relationships and bottom line. Focus on the outcome of change, not the activities needed to get there.

5. **Encourage Ownership of Change.** Employees must be included in the decisions about the change process at the earliest possible opportunity. No one wants to be forced to change; only those who feel heard and valued will willingly accept and adapt to the change. Inviting stakeholders into the change will diminish resistance to it.

6. **Mistakes Happen: Accept It, Encourage It, and Get Over It!** Lasting, effective, results-driven change doesn't take place without risk. Any change initiative is a risk; your employees must be allowed to take calculated risks, even if such gambles result in mistakes.

   The fear of mistakes and/or failure is at the heart of resistance to change. The most effective way to counter that resistance is to make it clear that you know mistakes will happen and they're part of the learning process. Real knowledge is never gained without mistakes.

7. **Out with the Old, In with the New... Maybe.** The more successful you are, the more rigid you can become in how you work and approach problems. As a leader in this rapid change environment, you must examine your old ways of doing business in light of new market forces. Don't hold onto to old patterns just because you are resistant to change.

   Look for ways to innovate, and be creative in devising new ways to solve today's business challenges. Let go where you need to, but only after a careful review of your options and methodologies. Being new and different doesn't always make it right, but tried-and-true may no longer work either.

8. **Celebrate Reincarnation.** You embarked on change for a reason: to be reincarnated! Celebrate this reincarnation and reward those who helped you get there. Encourage your employees to reinvent themselves on an individual scale, just as you reinvented the company together. Personal and professional growth is the result of constant learning and risk-taking. Those who eagerly embrace this knowledge and apply it to themselves will become your best leaders of change.

– The Other Kind of Change –

ACTION DRIVER ▶ *It's a Bitter Pill but You Still Gotta' Take It*

Stuff happens and so does change, sometimes when we least expect it and are least prepared.

A recent example occurred in my state – the takeover of Genzyme by Sanofi, the giant French pharmaceutical firm. Genzyme had to swallow a bitter pill – they were vulnerable with little ammunition to fight the unwanted advances of Sanofi and a takeover was virtually inevitable. Change was heading for them like an out of control nor'easter.

This very public struggle between the two aggressive CEOs of Genzyme and Sanofi is a great lesson about the obstacles to successful change. Here's what we can learn from their difficult battle:

- **Accept that Change Means "Letting Go" and that This Takes Time.** Genzyme's CEO, Henri Termeer, was not ready to let go of the company he had built. Change was more than just business to him - it was personal. It took almost nine months for him to emotionally accept the inevitable and truly negotiate the takeover.

  It is no different in your company. Accepting change is critical, but most companies ignore that aspect until they are deep into the change process. Why? Because it took them so long to realize that their resistance was due to their failure to acknowledge the change and let go of what was. Accepting change will take time – so accept that from the get-go. The more self-aware you and your company are, the shorter and less discomfiting the entire process will be.

- **Change is Always Personal.** No amount of assurance from management will erase all the personal insecurities around change. Your staff needs to hear those assurances, but as their leader, you need to give <u>individual</u> assurance, support, and coaching to each employee, and you must watch for signs that personal attacks are about to emerge. Termeer and his Sanofi counterpart spent months hurling barbs at each other in the press, further personalizing and complicating negotiations.

- Resisting change is normal and the desire to demonize the people asking for change is also human. However, this avenue is <u>never</u> productive and almost always creates a destructive environment for the companies, their employees, and their customers.

- **Keep Your Enemies Closer.** As the struggle between Genzyme and Sanofi continued, Carl Icahn, business tycoon and Genzyme shareholder, actively supported the takeover in direct opposition to Termeer. What did Termeer do? Well, he took a bold strategic step and gave Icahn two seats on the Genzyme board! The lesson: don't ignore your "resisters"; submerge them in the process.

Whether employees or managers, include detractors on your committees, seek their input, and work to win them over – or at the very least to neutralize their effect. The closer you keep the resisters to you, the more control you can exert.

- **Communication is Key to Successful Change.** Throughout the ordeal between Genzyme and Sanofi, the two CEOs communicated mainly through advisors. They avoided direct communication for months. It was only when they began talking to each other that the climate improved and negotiations became fruitful.

During change, it is especially critical for senior management to communicate directly with employees. Emails and proclamations from HR or Marketing will do nothing to build a bridge between the architects of change and those who must implement (and live with) it. Develop your communication plan before you announce change – **how you begin the change initiative sets its tone**. Open, honest communication must continue throughout the initiative from top-down and bottom-up. I can't stress enough how vital communication is to building and sustaining the trust required for change to succeed.

With negotiations over, Sanofi swallowed Genzyme and the real change work began. Given their vastly different cultures, both companies saw a very difficult time ahead with no assurances that the gains they hoped to achieve would ever be realized. When you and your company are faced with change, look around at others who have weathered similar storms and search for the lessons that will ease your course to successful change.

– Deep Dives –

Talent Management

To learn more about the concepts discussed in the Talent Management chapter of *Brick Wall Breakthrough*, consult these texts:

The 12 Absolutes of Leadership, Gary Burnison (2011, McGraw-Hill).

The Basics of Process Mapping, Robert Damelio (2009, Productivity Press).

Beyond Change Management: How to Achieve Breakthrough Results Through Conscious Change Leadership, Dean Anderson, Linda Ackerman Anderson (2010, Pfieffer).

Blink: The Power of Thinking Without Thinking, Malcolm Gladwell (2007, Back Bay Books).

Business Process Mapping: Improving Customer Satisfaction, J. Mike Jacka, Paulette J. Keller (2009, Wiley).

Change or Die: The Three Keys to Change at Work and in Life, Alan Deutschman (2007 HarperBusiness).

Change Your Questions, Change Your Life: 10 Powerful Tools for Life and Work, Marilee G. Adams, Ph.D. (2009, Berrett-Koehler Publishers).

Brick Wall Breakthrough

Crucial Conversations: Tools for Talking When the Stakes are High,
Kerry Patterson, Joseph Grenny, Ron McMillan, Al Switzler (2011,
McGraw-Hill).

Exploring Productivity, The Network for Productivity Excellence (2007,
Dawson).

The Five Dysfunctions of a Team: A Leadership Fable, Patrick Lencioni
(2002, Jossey-Bass).

Harvard Business Review's 10 Must Reads on Leadership, Harvard Business Review (2011, Harvard Business Review Press).

Hiring for Attitude: A Revolutionary Approach to Recruiting and Selecting People with Both Tremendous Skills and Superb Attitude, Mark A.
Murphy (2011, McGraw-Hill).

Influencer: The Power To Change Anything, Kerry Patterson, Joseph Grenny, David Maxfield, Ron McMillan, Al Switzler (2007, McGraw-Hill).

The Introverts Guide to Success in Business and Leadership, Lisa Petrilli
(2011, C-Level Strategies).

Leadership and Self Deception: Getting Out of the Box, Arbinger Institute
(2010, Berrett-Koehler Publishers).

Leadership by the Book: Tools to Transform Your Workplace, Ken Blanchard,
Bill Hybels, Phil Hodges (1999, William Morrow).

LEAN Six Sigma for Service: How to Use LEAN Speed and Six Sigma Quality to Improve Service and Transactions, Michael L. George (2003, McGraw-Hill).

LEAN Six Sigma Pocket Toolbook: *A Quick Reference Guide to 100 Tools for Improving Quality and Speed*, Micheal George, John Maxey, David Rowlands, Mark Price (2004, McGraw-Hill).

Managing Change and Transition,   Richard Lueke (2003, Harvard Busi-ness Review Press).

Managing Transitions: Making The Most of Change, William Bridges (2009, De Capo Lifelong Books).

One Page Talent Management: Eliminating Complexity, Adding Value, Marc Effron, Miriam Ort (2011, Harvard Business Review Press).

Powerhouse: Creating the Exceptional Workplace, Nancy Mobley (2011, Insight Performance).

Quick Hits: 10 Key Surgical Strike Actions to Improve Business Process Improvement, Kelvin F. Cross (2003, AMACOM).

Quiet Leadership: Six Steps to Transforming Performance at Work, David Rock (2007, Harper Business).

Strengths Based Leadership: Great Leaders, Teams, and Why People Follow, Tom Rath, Barry Conchie (2009, Gallup).

Switch: How to Change Things When Change is Hard, Chip Heath, Dan Heath (2010, Crown Business Press).

Brick Wall Breakthrough

The Talent Edge: A Behavioral Approach to Hiring, Developing, and Keeping Top Performers, David S. Cohen (2011, Wiley).

The Truth About Thriving in Change, William S. Kane (2008, FT Press).

– Conclusion –

Lessons from a Talk Show Host

The Big Reveal: Become Your Customer

Think like them, act like them. Understand, really understand, what your customers want, need, and desire. Your clients should drive every aspect of your company. Don't just build your products or services to their needs (that's a *duh!*), but create processes around how they want to do business with you.

Design a support system that provides true support and real solutions. Jettison those customer care people who can't solve anything without asking their supervisor, who make the customer feel like they're an interruption or – even worse – like they have the intelligence of a gnat! And by the way, your customers also know when that CSR is Raj in India, not Bernice in Peoria!

Need a great example of why the customer is the reason we exist – look to Ellen Degeneres's show. As a business, *Ellen* succeeds not only because of Ellen herself, but because of five key practices the show utilizes which, if adopted, will drive success for you too.

The 5 Key Business Success Drivers:

1. **Know Thy Customer.** Ellen understands, cares about, and identifies with her audience, i.e., her customers. Every element of the show is designed to answer and appeal to her customers' need

for fun, excitement, and exploration of new ideas, technologies, and issues. She believes in the intelligence of her audience and acts accordingly.

Become *customer-driven* not just customer-focused. Every company these days says they are customer-focused. Big deal! I'm "exercise-focused," but that sure as hell doesn't mean I consistently exercise. Being customer-driven demands that you build the department or company from the inside out to meet your customer's needs, not just to make life easier for you or your staff. How easy is it to order from you or sign a service contract with you? Would your customer describe your invoicing as clear, concise, complete, and understandable? Ask these kinds of questions, then answer them with solutions that satisfy your customer.

2. **Give 'Em Positive Surprises.** Want to build customer loyalty? Give them unexpected surprises – yes, I know, this is redundant. But it's also important. Consistency can breed compliancy, so the goal with surprises is to keep the customer coming back. Surprise your client with flowers or a coupon on the anniversary of their first purchase or contract signing. Better yet, acknowledge important dates in their business, like the day they opened or first served one million customers. Get creative and look for ways to positively impact their day: surprise them with an introduction to someone who would be a great prospect for their business, or a lunch party for their staff. Anything that celebrates your relationship with them will reinforce that relationship.

3. **Keep it Real, Keep it Honest.** Ellen Degeneres is viewed as open and honest. Some would describe her as courageous. Her audiences trust her because she trusts them. She honors and believes in their

intelligence. Ellen's self-effacing humor builds a feeling of safety, that she is just like her audience members, facing the same daily problems and admiring the same stories, even though she is famous.

How honest is your marketing material? How honest is your sales team? Does it stretch the truth about your product's or service's performance? Do you own up to mistakes quickly and resolve them without a lot of kicking and screaming by your customer? Letting your customers know you face the same realities, and being forthright and honest about your shortcomings will strengthen your relationships with them.

4. **Get a Sense of Humor.** It's obvious that *Ellen* is all about humor – about having fun! When was the last time you said, "This is fun!" when talking about your business? How about your staff – would they say it's fun to come to work?

   It better be. Because when things are not fun, your customers feel it, your employee turnover rate skyrockets, and your stress level becomes intolerable. Working hard is not the antithesis of enjoyment. Visitors to your office should hear more than the click of the keyboard or the clank of a printer. They should hear laughter.

5. **Dance as If No One is Watching.** It's a phrase Ellen has perfected. She begins almost every show by dancing to music she loves, as if millions of people weren't watching. With this simple act, Ellen speaks volumes:

- <u>Taking chances is okay</u>. Everyday Ellen tells her audience, i.e., her customers, that moving out of your comfort zone is not only okay, but can bring you camaraderie and success. Sometimes you have to take risks to get rewards.

- <u>Don't take yourself too seriously</u>. Ellen knows what's really important in life, and feeding an ego shouldn't be a top priority.
- <u>Have fun</u>. Having fun should be part of life, whether it's personal or in business. More importantly, Ellen's dancing tells us that we need to make our own fun because the rewards of doing so are immeasurable.

In ways big and small, every day *Ellen* demonstrates that it is all about the customer. This is the lens through which I hope you build, manage, and sustain your business. It is the underlying truth in the wisdom of this book.

– Acknowledgments –

It would take several lifetimes to repay Jonathan (Jeb) Bates for the contributions he has made to my life and career. Friend, colleague, mentor, creative genius - only partially describe the roles Jeb has played. Thank you for always being there when I needed an answer, a hug, or a kick in the a**!

Ken Lizotte of Emerson Consulting and his dedicated colleagues at thoughtleading.com started me on my path to authorship – sorry Ken that it took so long to write the book! Ken, Elena Petricone, and Kate Hannisian promoted my articles, white papers, and speaking engagements and became missionaries for "customer-focused management" – thank you doesn't capture how I feel about your support, advice, and expertise!

It took two editors to take my volume of writing and turn it into a book. Fran Snider, the "kool skater," willingly accepted the tough job of editing the first round and throwing out the superfluous. Her great work was followed by Jennie Cook of Blue Dog Editing (www.bluedogediting. com) who turned the manuscript into something worthy of being called a book.

Many thanks to Carolyn Wirth, artist, sculptor, and illustrator, who applied her considerable artistic talent to the creation of all artwork and illustrations (carolynwirthdesign.wordpress.com).

Brick Wall Breakthrough

According to the experts, great covers sell books. David Gillis of David Gillis Design nailed it with a fabulous cover design. Thanks David for translating my vision into a powerful visual message both inside and outside of the book (www.davidgillis design.com). Thank you for sharing your rare creative gift.

Infinite gratitude to Vicki Mills of Concord Web Solutions (www.concordwebsolutions.com) who dedicated her marketing talent to all aspects of my business and this book. She has generously shared her creativity and considerable marketing wisdom and has become a treasured friend.

Never ending thanks to family, friends, and clients who cajoled, begged, nagged, and pushed me to finally write *Brick Wall Breakthrough*. Everyone should be lucky enough to have people who so willingly share their time, advice, and love!

FAST FINDER

– Fast Finder –

The following index is organized by a "business challenge" you may be facing. Each challenge will direct you to the solution(s) for it.

Brick Wall Breakthrough

– About the Author –

Shelley Hall is Principal/Managing Director of Catalytic Management, LLC, a leading management consulting firm that produces critical transformational changes in the key areas of sales, customer service, change management, and process improvement. As a highly-successful entrepreneur and corporate fugitive who has built, reinvented, and turned around numerous companies, Hall is considered a leading expert in the field of customer-focused management. Over her 30-year career, Hall has held senior level positions in sales and management with companies in technology, education, advertising, and Internet sales. A thought leader and engaging speaker, she writes frequently for major business journals such as *Business Performance Management Magazine*, *CEO Refresher*, *The Handbook of Business Strategy*, *Women's Business*, *Manage Smarter,* and *Sales and Service Excellence.* Shelley is a mediocre golfer, a determined gardener, and, according to her family, insane for forsaking her Miami birthright and moving to Boston.

– About Catalytic Management, LLC –

Founded in 2001, Catalytic Management helps large and small companies kick-start performance and accelerate growth. We are seasoned experts in sales performance, customer service, process improvement, and change management – in other words, we help solve your company's most intractable business challenges.

Catalytic Management offers clients a remarkable lens through which to see your organizational systems in a heightened, more magnified form; to see – as many of our clients tell us –"what we could never see before."

Our consultants "have been there, done that." We bring a fresh new perspective, the management tools, and the knowledge necessary to understanding the myriad of issues confronting businesses today and tomorrow.

At Catalytic Management, we know that:

- Sales team productivity is the engine that drives growth
- Delivering great customer service makes money
- With change management, it's all about the people
- Process improvement doesn't have to be difficult or disruptive

Our mission is to unleash powerful forces of change for our clients. That's why we call our process and our company *catalytic*. Just like a chemical process when a new agent is introduced into the mix, the results are powerful and immediate. Our client's peace of mind comes from the sustainable results we deliver – not instant, off-the-shelf solutions! When working with Catalytic Management, new ideas and solutions begin to emerge for clients, ones that produce critical transformational changes

Brick Wall Breakthrough

in the key areas of sales, customer service, change management, and process improvement.

CPSIA information can be obtained at www.ICGtesting.com
Printed in the USA
BVOW04*1345091014

370093BV00002B/3/P